nappy

Growing
Up
Black
and
Female
in
America

Published for **Harlem River Press** by:
Writers and Readers Publishing, Inc.
P.O. Box 461, Village Station
New York, New York 10014

Cover and Book Design: Terrie Dunkelberger

ISBN: 0-86316-322-X

0 9 8 7 6 5 4 3 2 1

Manufactured in the United States of America

Growing
Up
Black
and
Female
in
America

nappy

aliona l. gibson

HARLEM RIVER PRESS

This book is
dedicated to every
person in my life,
past & present, who
has encouraged me
to write.

acknowledgments

I wish to give a most sincere thanks to my publisher Glenn Thompson for creating a space in the publishing world, where people like me can see their dreams become a reality. Thanks for believing in my work enough to take the risk. I feel very honored to be part of the 20th anniversary year of the Writers and Readers Publishing.

Thanks to Deborah Dyson whose enthusiasm about the book kept it alive for me and thanks to the rest of the Writers and Readers staff.

Thanks to my editors Neeti Madan and Patricia Allen.

Thanks to my entire family (especially my grandmothers Eloise Gibson & Jessie B. Robinson) and all of my friends for their love and support over the years.

Special thanks to all of my homegirls who had to deal with me during the course of this project, thanks for your love, words of encouragement and friendship: Tonya Anderson, Lisa Celaya, Anthea Charles, Rosalyn Coleman, Nyla Dyson, Shiree Dyson, Alison Fletcher, Tonya Hyder, Karna Leggett, Boo Peters, Aziza Reid, Angela Winn, Scottie Workman. And of course to my "other mothers": Melody Graham, Joy Harris, Paulette Houston, Elaine Lee, Jean Perkins.

Thanks to the few chosen people whom I let read what I had written well before it even became "a book": Dee Darby-Harper, Beverly Scott, Shanna at Marcus Bookstore in Oakland and Detra R. Woodard (my friend of seventeen years). Thanks to Evelyn C. White for introducing me to Flight of the Mind, where I learned the power of truth-telling.

-Aliona L. Gibson

contents

preface

In the tradition of African storytelling, my initial idea for *Nappy: Growing Up Black & Female in America* was derived from my own storytelling experiences. Anyone who knows me and even those who have only met me once or twice will tell you that I always have a story to tell. Most of the ones in this collection have been told countless times. I believe that they tell of intricate parts of my character and have managed to mold the person I am (and am becoming, as I consider myself a "work in progress").

I first realized how important cataloguing my experiences were, when I found my old diary about seven years ago. I couldn't believe what I had written and how much I had changed. My initial thought was to throw it away (as in "get rid of it quick!"), but then I decided that it was proof of my personal growth and something to be proud of, not embarrassed by. Finding the old diary was enough to inspire me to begin keeping a journal again. Occasionally, I'll read over old journals from previous years. Sometimes it's fun and interesting, and sometimes it's not; to see that you are still tripping over something that bothered you a year ago is not very encouraging.

At this point in my life, I feel I've reached the end of my youthful development. I try very hard not to get tied up in the "age issue." That, in addition to many other concepts, we've accepted from white people. In African societies, elders have always been the wisest and most respected individuals of the community. As a black woman, I should look forward to getting older. My mother and grandmothers have proved that we are like good wine and get better with age. Twenty-seven finds me closing out one era and coming into another. I know that I am "maturing," not just because the people I'm meeting these days are married, have been married or have children, but because my priorities are changing. I'm giving thought to things that I didn't think about before: What am I going to do with the rest of my life? And how am I going to achieve success?

Before writing *Nappy*, I had reached a point in my life where I felt stagnant. I was not being productive. I needed to do something that would yield a consequence—a finished product that I could actually hold in my hands—and would allow me to express myself creatively at the same time. Thus, *Nappy* was born.

These stories are a select few concerning the many persons and events that have made life more interesting for me. The views expressed are entirely my personal opinion, some of which are broad generalizations. I hope you will empathize and enjoy these experiences.

-Aliona L. Gibson

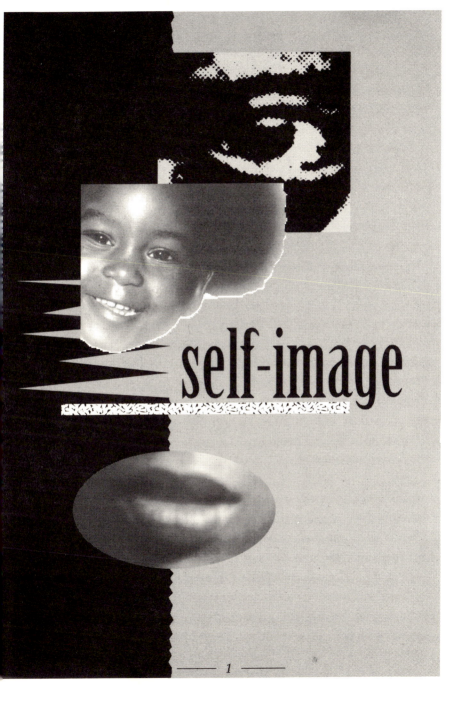

self-image

hair peace

I n a recent conversation with a stranger on the bus who decided to make my hair her business, I was reminded that it had been well over a year since I cut my hair off. I was amazed that so much time had passed. I guess I'd been so busy enjoying my "new look" that there hadn't been time to look back. I could only see the worry-free years ahead as I sported my short afro.

My life had been filled with a variety of transitions and accomplishments: Having graduated from college (being the first in my family to do so), and having moved across the country, I was learning to come to terms with my own needs rather than those of others. "My own needs," in this case, refer to my determining my self-image as a black woman. When it comes to beauty and self-image, women are socialized to doing things according to the whims of others—others being men—and not themselves.

Black women, in particular, are faced with ancient standards of beauty.

When I decided to cut my hair, it was because I realized that I was not meant to have straightened hair—it's just not for me. Some people are better suited for (and far more attractive with) natural hair. *I* am one of those people! Every single time I've had my hair chemically treated, it's led to disaster. I insisted on learning the hard way that chemicals and my hair just don't belong together. It took several bad experiences for me to decide that I'd best stick with the hot comb, and anyone who has ever had their hair pressed can imagine what a terrible inconvenience that is. In retrospect, I think my hair was telling me to cut it all off, but I ignored the signs and continued torturing my hair.

It all started when I was four years old. I had a massive head of long, thick, uncontrollable hair that was more than a notion to comb and, God forbid, to wash. At the age of four, I got my hair pressed for the first time, which made combing my hair more an act of grooming and less one of abuse. Pressing my hair became a way of life—visits to the hairdresser every other week for the next seven or eight years. It wasn't until I was twelve and got my first perm that trouble erupted.

A week after I got the perm, I dreamt that I woke up and all of my hair was on the pillow! Now that I think about it, that was probably the first sign of many hair troubles ahead. Six months into my life of permed hair, the area around my temples started shedding and eventually—not my whole head, just the temple area—became bald !

Yes, like the back of your hand.

After that disaster, I turned back to the hot comb. And then the Jheri Curl came out. I, of course, got the curl, and my hair grew like crazy—for the first year. It wasn't until I decided that I wanted versatility that the problems began. In my attempt to wear it blow dried, I once again faced serious hair loss. So I decided on extensions until it grew back, at which point I returned to the straightening comb. During this time I got my hair cut in layers, a "snatch-back." It was really cute for two or three days after leaving the salon. The other week and a half between visits, I'd pull it back in a tired ponytail, my trademark through my high school years. Now getting my hair pressed every two weeks and rolling it up every night was not my idea of how a young woman of the '80s was supposed to live. I thought that this was probably just fine back in the '50s, when we didn't have alternatives, but in the '80s this is *not* happenin'! This attitude allowed me to be coerced into trying the "curly perm" once again. No need to re-describe my travesties. But this time was worse than before, because the woman braiding my hair informed me that, had it been any shorter, she would not have been able to add the extensions. So, I resorted to braids again (and later the press-n-curl) and vowed never to put another chemical in my hair.

As a college senior, my bi-monthly visits to the hair dresser were too costly and time consuming. So, I opted for braids again, this time with my own hair, no extensions. I expected it to braid well since all of the chemically treated hair was either burned out or had fallen out. I thought it would curl up on the ends like regular, kinky, black hair does in it's natural state. WRONG !!! I ended up with one-hundred bone-straight, toothpick-looking plaits. They poked out all over my head like I had just stuck my finger into an electric socket. That was the last straw!

Every bad hair experience I'd ever had came to mind on that day, and I was practically in tears. I was frustrated and simply disgusted. From years of pressing and chemicals, my hair was ruined. It had died a second death. Ironically enough, I was writing my thesis on American standards of beauty and their effect on women of color. My section on black people and our hair, coupled with my experience, was enough to convince me to cut mine off.

In the twenty-four hours between the time I got the plaits and the time I cut it all off, I thought about all of the things I'd have to deal with: being mistaken for a lesbian; being, supposedly, an expert on black history and culture; fighting off white men and their damn "jungle fever"; and, oh, the "biggie," hanging up the idea of having a black boyfriend—just a few of the stigmas and nuances that come with wearing your hair short and natural as a black woman in America. I decided that being able to wash my hair whenever I wanted, and finally being able to learn to swim were more important to me than other people's hang ups.

It never really bothered me that I couldn't swim until I went to Kenya in 1985. There I was in Mombassa, a gorgeous paradise of a city on the east coast of Africa, facing the beautiful Indian ocean, stifled by my inability to dive head first into the water. It was the most incredible setting I'd ever seen: the ocean water was aqua blue—about eighty degrees, white sand, palm trees, and beautiful black people everywhere. For fear of drowning, I could only wade into the water. Every time I had gotten up enough nerve to take a swimming course, I was in one of my "remission" stages, which meant I was getting my hair pressed. I was not about to jump in some fool's pool and end up having to put out seventy-five dollars to get my hair re-done three times a week or burning it out myself, which I'd proven to be pretty good at in the past. The decision was clear. I'd have to wait until my hair could stand a perm before I would learn to swim, which, I thought at the time, might be never.

I'd made up my mind, and it seemed the only logical thing to do. Sheila Head (a well-known hair sculptress in Oakland) gave me a cut that was more to my character than any bob, snatch-back, flip, or curl could ever be. She made it look as though I had been wearing a natural for years. I loved it right away and felt really good knowing that I was neither embarrassed nor afraid to let everybody see what my "real" hair looks like. I'd decided to liberate myself and do what was best for me. Reactions were the most interesting part of it all, some people suggesting that I relax it "a little" to get that "curly look." I just rolled my eyes and thought to myself—If they only knew.... At the same time, I had older black women telling me what a pretty face I had and how well my hair suited me.

From friends and family, there were both positive and negative reactions. But regardless of what anybody said, I was happy with my decision. For black folks, hair styling is a major aspect of our grooming, but I can honestly say I felt more attractive with none. I wore clothes and colors I wouldn't have dreamed of wearing before. It was exactly what I needed to come out of my shell and to look and feel the best that I possibly could. It's amazing what changing your hair can do. I only wish I had made this decision years before. I hoped I would have enough courage to continue to live for myself, making decisions that would suit my own needs rather than those of others.

One afternoon I was waiting in line to go through the turnstile at the subway station when a West Indian man made a comment that embarrassed me and had everybody within earshot laughing at me. We got to the turnstile at the same time, and in a loud voice he said that he was trying to figure out whether I was a boy or a girl. I didn't exactly find the comment amusing, but it didn't convince me to go out and buy big earrings or start wearing lipstick. I knew I was comfortable having short hair, and I knew I didn't look like a boy. My roommate Jerina (who also had a short natural but had been wearing one at Berkeley High years before it became trendy) told me that her boyfriend loved her hair short but insisted that she not leave the house without at least lipstick on. He preferred both earrings and lipstick, but if she was just going to the corner store or something like that just lipstick was fine. (Amazing, huh?) I got tired of

everybody suggesting I wear big earrings, implying that I needed them so people would know I was female. I almost started to buy some when I realized that I have never liked wearing big earrings, they're just not my style.

At the other end of the spectrum, I met my friend Michael because of my hair—or lack thereof. I was walking down the street in East Harlem, minding my own business, as always, when he came running up to me out of nowhere, took one look at me and felt compelled to tell me how beautiful he thought I looked with my hair short and natural. He proceeded to follow me to the bus stop and waited with me, all the while engaging me in a conversation about black women and our hair. He told me how nice it was to see a sister who didn't accept the media standards of beauty, which for us required having long hair. It was a good conversation. Michael was cute and charming. He asked me for my phone number, but it would be six months and two meetings later that I would finally give it to him. He seemed like a nice guy, but I guess I was thinking that Melody would kill me if she knew I was even *talking* to strange men on the street, let alone giving one my phone number.

Let me tell you a little about Melody. She was one of the many women in my life who provided me with the guidance and support necessary to survive college life and to my becoming a woman. Just like the other women who would become mentors to me, she was from the east coast and encouraged me to get out of California for a while. She came out west from New York to go to law school at U.C. Berkeley. She seemed so perfect to me—the quintessential independent black woman of the '80s, a true *Essence* woman. She was the kind of woman a young girl could look at and say, "I want to be like her when I grow up."

One of my more typical encounters with my short natural took place when I went into the ladies room at a night club. Usually packed, the mirror would be filled with women whose hair "fell" from the heat and humidity of the club. No matter how hard I danced or how much I would sweat, my hair was the *least* of my concerns. I'd take a quick glance in the mirror to put on more lipstick, if I was even wearing any, and be on my way. Inevitably someone would say, "your hair looks cute like that, but you're skinny so you can wear it." Or, "I like your hair, but I could never cut all mine off. I just don't look right with short hair." And occasionally I'd get,
"What made you cut your hair off like that?"

People would comment as if they knew me before I cut my hair and as if I had had long, beautiful, healthy hair. Some people would rather have long, unhealthy, dead hair than a short, healthy head of hair. It's strange, but I think it's indicative of our obsession with long hair. I often hear people with dreadlocks talk about all the negative comments they got when they first started to develop their locks, but the minute their locks became shoulder length attitudes changed.

I enjoyed my new look until one day I got bored, needed a change, and had to figure out what to do next. For the first time in my life I felt like my options were endless. After wearing my hair natural for three years and two months, I knew I enjoyed not worrying about getting my hair wet or getting nappy edges from washing my face or getting a facial. I loved having so little hair, and I was sure that I would miss the convenience of being able to groom it with three strokes of a brush. My days of being able to wake up, get dressed, get half way down the block, and realize that I forgot to comb my hair would be over. I had absolutely no desire to wear my hair straightened, so *that* was out of the question.

I'd had several lengths, shapes, and styles during the three years that I sported my afro and had gotten to the point where I would go to Turning Heads in Harlem and just let Justo do his thing. No more "shorter on the sides, tapered at the neck, long on top, rounded, not square, etc." The fate of my head was in the hands of this Puerto Rican man, whose straight hair prompted me at first sight to think, "No way—what does he know about naps?" I let this man shave my head into a "light Caesar," and to my surprise, I loved it. It was certainly a *change*. On the other hand,

I never *did* get used to strange men taking it upon themselves to rub my head, talking about how nicely shaped it was.

Initially, I worried about what I would do with my hair when I got bored or tired of this style. One of my first thoughts was, "Oh, my God, what about that in between stage when it's too long for some styles and too short for others, what will I do then?" It was about to become a real dilemma for me until I took the advice (for the umpteenth time) of my friend Paulette. She knows me very well and understands my tendency to worry. She told me to cross that bridge when I got to it.

At the point when I decided not to cut my hair anymore and let it grow, my homegirl from Harlem, Aziza, showed me how to wrap my head with African fabric. I got to the point where I was making weekly visits to the fabric store buying material for my head to match my clothes. I realized how such a thing could be addicting—the head wrap had become a regular part of my wardrobe. As soon as my hair got long enough, I wore it in "twisties." I graduated from those to micro braids, with just my own hair, no extensions. Finally, my hair was acting the way it was supposed to, the way I had expected it to years before in it's natural state. This was an easy style and looked adorable. The only draw back was that I got sick and tired of everybody wanting to know if I was "dreading," which, when I do decide to do it, will not be because of a trend or a fad.

So everything is going fine, and I'm loving my hair for about the second time in my life, then, BAM! In my state of joblessness, I luck upon an interview with a prestigious art institution. Great pay, full benefits, in the arts, and a position in my field (public relations). The job was perfect, and I considered it mine. But, of course, I needed to figure out what to do with my hair. For those of you who don't know, twistie/dreadlocked and braided hairstyles pose potential problems. Case in point: In 1981, Dorothy Reed, a popular Bay Area television personality was suspended from her job as a local T.V. anchor for wearing her hair in braids. I'm still trying to figure out what her hairstyle had to do with how she performed her job. Anyway, she's been on the radio ever since.

On the recommendation of someone who knew the inside scoop at the institution where I was to interview, I got my hair pressed. Her advice was to "get the job first, then do whatever you want with your hair." I spent forty dollars and two-and-a-half hours getting my hair ready to interview—all this for a job that I might not get. It was an experience that I could have easily gone without. I had finally had my head of virgin hair, and there I was letting this man run a smoke-filled comb through my wonderfully nappy coif.

Well—I didn't get the job. Someone snidely commented that I might have been hired if I hadn't "compromised my values" and pressed my hair for the interview. Just because I had a natural, and I like my hair in it's natural state, doesn't mean that I have a problem with straightened hair. For me, cutting my hair was just another option. In terms of our hair, I think that's what it should be all about: whatever makes you feel good and whatever works for you. I happen to be a "low maintenance" person, so the natural was the best thing I could have done for myself. All this is to say that as much as I get bored and have a need for change, straight hair will probably be an option for me at some point in my life.

So, then, I got extensions, shoulder-length, braided individuals. Every other time I've had braids it's been corn rows. I'm just a tad too conservative to have long hair that's store bought. Two women that I know were laughing at me, basically calling me a hypocrite for having extensions since I'm so hard on people with weaves and fake hair. The situation was totally bizarre, because, one, I would be the first one to tell you that this is not my real hair: "For God's sake, it was made in China." I was not embarrassed by my "real" hair or trying to hide it like a lot of people who sport weaves. I don't need "long hair" to feel pretty, nor do I have a problem with shaving my head, which, now that I know I'm not afraid to do so, is a viable option for me. Two days after I got braids I got a call for another job interview. It's funny how things work out sometimes. I had a great interview and got the job, but I still wonder whether I would have been hired with my twisties.

> *I've heard it and never wanted to believe it, but I guess it's true: Men are so much more attracted to women with "long hair."*

I got all kinds of attention and compliments when I had my hair braided with extensions. Imagine that! They didn't give me the time of day with my short natural, not in Oakland anyway. Are the brothers that shallow? I couldn't believe it. Synthetic hair

—— 13 ——

from China attached to my own hair made me more desirable to men. With my hair in braids, I got hair compliments, winks, and suggestive smiles from men. Some guys didn't even know they were extensions, which I found hard to believe. "I bet your hair is real long when it's not braided," this man once told me. I was quick to bust his bubble. In my most sarcastic manner I responded, "Nope, it's about as long as yours." He bugged. "That's not your real hair?" I was like, "No, I had a short natural, and I'm growing it out. My hair is less than an inch long." He was shocked and amazed and couldn't take his eyes off my head for the rest of the conversation. I'd always be all open and nonchalant about the fact that the braids were not my real hair when it came up. I thought his reaction was hilarious, so I liked having braids.

I really enjoyed not having to comb my hair for months at a time. The only drawback with braids was that I was afraid they would pull my hair out and break off around my temples. Next to having a bad perm job that results in bald patches that look like mange, *this* has to be the absolute worse! Unfortunately, there are a lot of women walking around whose hair line is completely gone. I don't want to be one of those people. It's not a pretty sight. When I see people like that I want to say, "Just cut it all off, and start over again. It's not so bad having short hair. It would look so much better, really."

> *It's interesting that there can be different degrees of how things affect us.*

During one of our many hair conversations, I told my friends that I remember having, as an adolescent, one of those blonde haired, blue-eyed doll heads, the kind they use in cosmetology school. I loved that thing and would spend hours on end making up new hairstyles. I especially enjoyed being able to wet her hair, not having to worry about combing it before it dried nor risk breaking the teeth of the comb like I did with my own hair. I can't remember, I said, ever consciously wishing I was white, but if given the opportunity, I would have traded in my naps for hair like my doll's in a minute. Veronica said she never wanted hair like white people; she wanted long wavy, naturally curly "Puerto Rican" hair. The kind of hair black people still, in this day and age, refer to as "good hair." She said she remembered it being so gratifying when her grandmother told her she had a good "grade" of hair. I know someone who refused to cut her child's hair because she was hoping and praying that it would stay the texture it was when the child was born. The most ridiculous story I've ever heard in this regard is Ricky telling me how many women had sex with him because of his "good hair!"

"Good hair" shouldn't even be part of our vocabulary. Those same women would completely bug if they saw Ricky now, with his dreadlocks just past his shoulders. They look wonderful to me, but the kids he works with think he's from Jamaica and does voodoo. Ever since my "dead hair" experience, I consider my hair, in it's natural state, "good" hair, and yes, it can still easily break the teeth out of a comb.

All I want is flexibility and versatility. I would like to be able to do a lot of different things with my hair, and, as a black woman, I *do* have options: natural hair, permed/relaxed/texturized hair, short straight hair, short nappy hair, long nappy hair, braids, Senegalese twists, dreadlocks, pressed hair...the possibilities are endless, and when it comes to hair styling black women are creative geniuses. I've seen our women wearing some of the most beautiful hairstyles. But what I want the most is healthy hair, whether its long, short, natural, or straight. I want the kind of "good hair" Lonnice Brittenum Bonner describes in her book of the same name: "...hair that's healthy-looking, a natural adornment." That means hair that requires little or no heat (blow dryers, hot combs, hot curlers), chemicals (relaxers, curls), or too much gunky junk (Sta-Sof-Fro, Pro-line, Carefree Curl, World of Curls, Dixie Peach, Royal Crown, Ultra Sheen, Soft Sheen, etc.).

Hair is the black woman's obsession.
Well, I want to stop obsessing over "what to do next" with my head and start channeling my energy into developing other parts of who I am. I love my hair, and I feel like I have really grown to accept and appreciate it. Now, if I could feel as confident and comfortable with the rest of me, I'd have it going on.

body language

Body image, after hair stuff, is another "issue" for black women. Losing weight, one of the inevitable topics of discussion that comes up with us, gets real tired for me. I guess it would since I've never had a weight problem. Not to sound like it hasn't been or isn't an "issue" for me. I am living proof that even skinny people have body image problems. I'm trying to come to terms with the fact that an anorexic figure, like many other physical characteristics we admire, is a standard created by the white controlled media. I have what I think is a very typical body for black women, smaller on top and round and shapely on the bottom. I'm learning to accept the fact that everything I eat seems to gravitate to a single section of my body. I need to be giving thanks because sometimes I feel like if it wasn't for my ass, I'd probably be shapeless.

I would like to know why having a big booty is the butt of jokes (no pun intended)? I've noticed that whenever someone is making fun of a black woman it's because she has a big butt. Why is *that* so funny? It's kind of ironic, because I can't tell you how many times I've heard men talk about what a nice, big, juicy, round behind a certain woman has, and I *still* haven't figured out what an "ass like butter" is. What I *do* know is that in my experience, black men (that's all I ever deal with, so I can't speak of anyone else) like big butts. Some don't though, they like that "ironing board" action. Even though it's a desired physical attribute, a lot of women speak of needing to lose weight, and the two "problem" areas are hips and booty. I get particularly disturbed by the fact that there are women beyond the age of adolescence who *still* complain and freak out about having a big butt. My own circle of friends have to listen to my declaration: "I hate to be the bearer of bad news, but you're a woman of African descent and booty comes with the territory." Sometimes I just say what Phyllis Yvonne Stickney would say: "There's power in the boo-tay!" I, personally, see it as something to be proud of, it's one of those many things that makes us unique. Unfortunately, having a different shape and form is not looked upon in a positive light in America. You can either live with that notion, despising your God-given temple until you die, or take a critical look at the situation and learn to love and appreciate your own beautiful self.

W hite America's standard of a "good body" is the complete opposite of what it is in the black community. Yet it's supposed to be a compliment when a friend tells me how "lucky" I am to be so skinny... "girl, if I had your shape..." or "if I was your size...." The sad part is that it's usually coming from some woman who has the kind of body that makes me wish we could trade or borrow the way we do with clothes. On two occasions a couple of my friends told me that if they had my figure, they would walk around naked. "The grass is always greener ...." Sometimes I feel like I would give anything to have a "brick house" body. You know, 36-24-36. I want to be able to fill out a form-fitting dress the way sistas did in the '50s. But in my quest for self-acceptance, I try to be grateful for what I have. It's an odd thing, but I've yet to meet a single woman who is completely satisfied with her body or the way she looks. We have a name for you women out there who would not change a thing about the way you look—*DIVA*!

> *A white woman's worse nightmare is a black woman's best and most prominent physical attribute: hips and ass.*

It wasn't always that way; the turn-of-the-century bustle was quite a hit. And I always thought that, for a white woman, Marilyn Monroe had a fly shape. Of course, if she were around today, she would be sent straight to Jenny Craig. It's too bad, because I think it's normal for women to have *some* body fat. We're supposed to have hips, breasts, thighs, and meat on our bones. I use Marilyn as an example because she was one of the people I most idolized and considered "beautiful."

Like every other child in America, I grew up being constantly bombarded with images of beauty that I couldn't relate to. My sense of my own beauty and self-image were formed by what I saw on television and by what I saw in teen magazines like *Seventeen* and *Mademoiselle*. The girls in those shows and in those magazines looked nothing like me, not even the black ones.

I can remember, as though it were yesterday, the period in my life when I began developing hips. I actually have it written in one of my old diaries, "I hate HIPS." What was I bugging on? I guess Farrah Fawcett, Kate Jackson, Jacqueline Smith, or Cheryl Ladd (*Charlie's Angels*) didn't have hips, and they were grown women. I just couldn't conceive of having hips, even though my mother, grandmothers, and aunts did. Back then I didn't get as sick as I do now when I watch TV or look in magazines, saying over and over to myself, "God, please tell me I do *not* look like that." For a while I was even wishing I had a brick on my night stand so when that Revlon "shake that body" commercial came on I would be ready. The commercial featured three little bony white girls that didn't have body the first! And it really bothered me that they were getting paid thousands (probably millions) of dollars perpetuating images that were messing women up and, even more important-ly, were bunk.

While I was feeling disgusted about my expanding hips, I also developed bad posture. In junior high school I was elected acting president of the "ittie-bittie-tittie-committee." I was constantly being teased about being flat-chested, and on occasion I'd get it from a family member. My stepfather once told me that I'd best keep my hair long, because if it wasn't for my hair nobody would be able to tell if I was a boy or a girl.

From a very early age, women are socialized to do things according to what pleases men; we grow up with the idea that we have to be pretty for them and not for ourselves. My desire for cleavage wasn't because I wanted to wear bustiers, halter tops, or strapless dresses—I've always been a pretty conservative dresser. I thought cleavage would make me look more like a woman. I'm amazed at how different kids are these days. I chaperoned a party for someone turning seventeen, and half the girls that came to the party made me and my friends look like the teenagers! At fifteen, sixteen and seventeen, they had titties and booty for days, the kind of bodies that I can only long for. We were only ten years older than them, but we kept saying, "Damn, we didn't look like that at their age." I blame it on the fortified Cheerios. I bugged off how comfortable and confident they seemed to be about their bodies. They were coming through in spandex, biker shorts, and hot pants, dressed for comfort and allure and not a bit embarrassed about it either!

Nowadays, comfort is first and foremost in my style of dress, which is why I don't even wear a bra half the time. You can never tell whether I have one on anyway, so I figure what's the point. Lately, though, I've been trying to remember to wear one, because I'm told I'll be sagging when I get older if I don't. Somehow I think that's going to happen regardless, for the same reason my behind won't be suspended in mid-air the way it is now when I'm 45. The bras I own are purely for aesthetic purposes; I buy and wear them because I think they look pretty. Unlike with my shoe size, I don't have to worry about Victoria's Secret being out of my bra size. The older I get the more appreciative I am of my small breasts, I actually enjoy the freedom and flexibility. I used to refer to myself as "flat-chested" until my senior year in college when I met a Korean woman who prayed for breasts my size. She'd been thinking about getting implants. More recently a close friend got a breast reduction. Usually I'm totally against any kind of plastic surgery but my friend's was not cosmetic, it was in the best interest of her health. In the best interest of mine, I have learned to stop complaining and be grateful for what I have. Besides, I think there are several other parts of my body that make up for any "lacking areas."

The thing I remember most about my body image and growing up, and more specifically how much I was tripping, is that wool coat that I used to wear. When I was about 12 or 13, in junior high school, I wore a long, full-length wool coat to school every-day for about a year. The coat had fur around the hood, sleeves, and hem. It covered my body from my neck to just below my knees. It was my security blanket, and while everyone else in my class hung their coats in the coat room, I kept mine on for the whole day, even while sitting at my desk. In the yearbook there is a photograph of me at my desk looking totally involved in whatever I was reading, tightly clinching my coat collar closed. I was totally embarrassed about the changes in my body, and my solution was to hide. In the years to come the long, wool coat would be replaced with baggy, over-sized clothes that made it difficult to decipher what was underneath. I was skinny and found myself being a little jealous of the girls with "normal" fig-ures, they seemed so much older and more mature than me and got more attention from the boys.

It's a strange experience to go into a store and not be able to find a pair of jeans that fit comfortably. I love Levi 501's, and at my size you wouldn't think I'd have a problem finding some that fit. Guess again. I have tried on and actually bought Gap classic fit jeans. The operative word in that description is "classic." Only recently have I begun to wonder who they design these jeans for? And what body type? These are very relevant questions. On countless occasions I have picked up what I thought was my size and was unable to get them up past my thighs. The ones that I can get past my hips and thighs are too tight across my butt (which smash my ordinarily round behind in) and are entirely too big in the waist. So you're probably thinking— that's what belts are for. Well, if you can stick your whole arm down the back of them when they're zipped and buttoned, they're probably not a good fit. I'm a size 5/6, and *I* have these problems. So I can't imagine what a larger sized woman must go through. Imagine that! Something as simple as buying a pair of jeans is enough to make you think there's something wrong with you— that you don't quite measure up for "classic" jeans.

In September 1991, I was urged to meet a friend of a friend of mine. A photographer living in New Jersey. Since I'm an amateur photographer, I called him up, had a great conversation, and agreed to pay him a visit. I spent the whole day at his studio/loft. He showed me a project he was working on called "Women of Color," a photographic exhibit celebrating the beauty and diversity of black and Hispanic women. The photos were nudes and showed the various physical attributes of women of color that are considered—by

American standards—"imperfections": small breasts, round booties, big thighs, etc. I saw the photographs and marveled at how he made each woman's body look like a work of art. He had a particularly good eye for displaying the individuality of each model. The photos glorified the bodies of black women the way TV and the mainstream print media glorify the bodies of white women. I couldn't think of anything in existence that celebrated the beauty of our bodies the way David's project did. The only thing remotely comparable on the market was what I considered a trashy book of photographs of African women taken by some German man who obviously had a "thing" for black women and our breasts and unfortunately had the resources to produce and market his work.

David asked me to pose, but I turned him down flat. I appreciated what he was doing and wanted to be supportive but not *that* damn supportive! Afterwards, I tried to figure out why I couldn't bring myself to do it: Was I ashamed of my body or embarrassed for him to see me with no clothes on? (I thought I'd dealt with that issue the year before when I saw a male gynecologist for the first time.) Did I not see my body as a work of art? Or was I more concerned about what other people thought of me?

> *Black people, contrary to popular belief, are a conservative lot.*

I worried about being labeled "loose" or a "freak" but then realized that anyone who spends seven or eight months out of the year being celibate couldn't possibly be "loose." The fact that I was living in New York, three thousand miles away from my family and close friends might have been another contributing factor in my decision. Plus, I began thinking: compared to what other people in the family are doing, this ain't shit. Smoking crack, robbing a store, lying, cheating and stealing from your relatives are all worse than taking a few pictures with your clothes off.

So, why was I still so apprehensive about posing? I was really relieved when my friend Shiree called me from California. "Girl, you should be flattered that somebody wants to use you to create something." Since I trust her judgment and I had admired his work, I followed her advise and allowed David to photograph me. And I'm so happy that I did. The photographs are wonderful. Of course, the ones I like the best weren't used for the exhibit. Looking at the 11X14 black and white photographs was like looking in a mirror, and I liked what I saw. I mostly liked the fact that I had enough courage and confidence about my body to go through with it.

Photo by David Booker

When I was a little girl my family used to call me "chicken legs." I've always been thin, but I bet never in a million years would they have guessed that I would grow up to have the legs I have now. One summer in N.Y. I was nicknamed "legs" by a guy in my neighborhood. The first time he saw me in shorts he came up to me and asked me, with a totally straight face, if my legs were real. I got the gift of gams from my grandmother and my mother, who both have legs to die for. I think my grandmother on my mom's side still has it going on. She probably had the kind of body when she was younger that I long for. I love my legs, and my mom tells me all the time that they are beautiful. Even strangers, men and women (straight or gay), compliment me on my legs. As a teenager I only wore long skirts. I had this thing for anything ankle length, practically every skirt I owned was long. When I finally did get around to wearing mini skirts, my mother used to embarrass me, going around telling everybody what gorgeous legs I had and how they ran in the family. Now, its rare to see me in anything even knee length. I show off my legs and don't think twice about spending a small fortune on legwear. I'm working on feeling as good about the rest of my body as I do about these legs.

Part of looking good is feeling good, from the inside out. Developing a sense of spirituality is a very valuable thing in this mad world we live in. A strong sense of self-worth and self-love is equally important. Feeling good about the person you are and feeling that you deserve the best that life has to offer is more than a notion for a lot of people. A positive self-image doesn't automatically come with age. It's not the sort of thing that is automatically transferred from parent to child either. There are so many other things in our society that have an influence on the way we see ourselves that it becomes almost impossible for a parent to be guaranteed that their child will maintain a sense of self in the real world.

nicki

A friend called me from L.A. the other day and during our conversation I nearly had a cow when she told me that her niece Nicki was on a Vanna White trip. She thought Vanna White was the most beautiful woman in the world. The most beautiful? In the world? It reminded me of my Marilyn Monroe craze, and I was thoroughly disgusted. Nicki is a cute brown-skinned girl with round, brown eyes and a button nose. She has a thick head of springy, tightly curled hair that's been straightened with a kiddy, no-lye perm. She has nappy edges and a "kitchen" from sweating, playing, and running wild.

Nicki is obviously the product of two people of African decent. There is no need to ponder or question her racial background. You are not reminded of the rape of black women during slavery or the white man's blood that flows through many of our veins, but is only more visible in some than in others. She is an undeniably black African-American girl. It shouldn't be surprising that someone who looks like Vanna White would appeal to her. How could it not? Everything in our society says that Vanna White equals real beauty: fair skin, long hair (blonde yet), small European facial features, and no ass. Oddly enough, these same characteristics are the complete opposite of those most black women possess. Granted, things have changed a little over the years but not enough. It's no accident that the world's highest paid black model owns fifty wigs. I think I took Nicki's Vanna White trip harder than her own family did. It's one of my issues—blacks considering whites more beautiful.

As sad as it may seem, Nicki is not alone in her admiration of white "beauty." In reference to the famous doll study, where black children were shown to have a preference for white dolls instead of black ones, bell hooks (in a recent lecture) sarcastically asked, "Did we have to do a 'study' to figure that out?" I couldn't help but think of the self-image and self-esteem problems this child would endure as a teenager and later as an adult if she is not straightened out now! These thought patterns need to be nipped in the bud, in fact, they shouldn't even become a bud. I thought about the fact that if she considered this blonde-haired, blue-eyed woman "beautiful," then how could she not look in the mirror and think there is something wrong with her. If *that* is her beauty ideal, then what does she make of her own dark skin, African facial features and kinky hair? How could this child possibly believe that she herself is beautiful?

For many African Americans, "beauty" constitutes being of mixed heritage or having a "mulatto" look. Have you ever noticed that whenever we talk about somebody who is beautiful or "fine," they have certain characteristics and a certain "look?" If that's the case, then what does that make the rest of us? Chopped liver? I think not. I refer to those of us who are undeniably black, "regular folks," and this does not strictly apply to those of us who happen to be dark-skinned, with African features and nappy hair. It has to do with what I think makes black people the most beautiful in the world. We come in all shades and hues, have a variety of facial features and various hair textures. People don't seem to realize the infinite number of possibilities that creates. Which should make it damn hard for us to "all look alike."

I don't believe that people who are mixed (or look as though they are) are somehow not black or black enough and can't represent black America. I would just like to see more accurate representation. I'm sure a lot of regular-looking black women appreciated Spike Lee's film *She's Gotta Have It,* which demonstrates that you don't have to be light-skinned, with hair down your back to be considered fine. For me, personally, the movie was a welcomed, long-awaited change of pace. If we want to see more of those kinds of positive images, we have to continue to make our own films. Things definitely change when you call your own shots.

I guess I should be happy that I wasn't born ten years earlier, when people who look like me were considered downright ugly. We were given "hope" with opportunities to change the way we look with a variety of beauty products that "guaranteed" good results. In my collection of *Ebony* magazines from the '50s, I was appalled and amazed by ads for beauty products promising the impossible: "Don't let your dark, drab skin rob you of romance. Have prettier, lighter skin in just seven days," or ads for a product promising to give you a better life by changing the texture of your hair, with a special formula for "extra stubborn" hair. In some of the ads they even used white people!!! If you have nappy hair, like the vast majority of black folks, no matter *what* kind of relaxer you use, or how *often* or how *much* you use, your hair would *never* be the texture of the hair in the ad. That's the problem with magazines; not only do they make you feel like there's something wrong with you to begin with, they have special marketing techniques that— ridiculous as they are—actually work on some people.

As an African-American woman who is "undeniably" black, I can say that—even though I didn't always feel this way—I *do* consider myself beautiful. Deep down I think I've always felt like I was pretty, but being brainwashed and bombarded with images of beauty that were the opposite of mine, I always found something that could be improved upon.

I can't remember ever hating everything about the way I looked or feeling jealous or less fortunate than people who happened to be born light-skinned. I did, however, come to the realization that light-skinned people, no matter what they looked like, were considered prettier (and thus the more sought after) than me.

It's amazing the kinds of things women who look like me have been (and are) subjected to. I am, nevertheless, sympathetic to the pain of light-skinned women, but I really don't think being occasionally called piss colored, half-white, zebra, or the like compares to being made to feel like you got beat with the ugly stick. I've had people apologize for describing me as "dark-skinned," as if it's a curse, or say things like "she's dark *but* pretty," as if you can't possibly be both.

I had quite a rude awakening recently when a woman I know told me that I was too black to date one of her sons. We were driving along in a car and started talking about having children. She was telling me about how when you decide to have children with someone you need to consider what they look like and what kind of child the two of you would produce together. I've never consciously given any thought to things like that, but I listened with curiosity. It intrigued me that she was so open and candid during the whole conversation. The more she talked, the more I started making up excuses for the ridiculous words that came out of her mouth. Then I realized that one watered-down margarita and a shot of cheap tequila could not account for her backward ideas about color. She went on to tell me that when she was growing up she had been encouraged to get together with men who were approximately the same complexion but definitely no darker. Her parents had instilled that idea in her, and she instilled it in her children. For several reasons it seemed very odd to me. First off, she wasn't that much lighter than me, and second, she was around my mother's age, so I didn't expect that mentality from someone of her generation. Plus she was from the east coast, not from the south or out west, where I think people are more color struck. She caught me totally off-guard. I was amazed by what she was saying. To get a better grasp, I asked, "So you wouldn't approve of one of your sons going out with someone who looked like me?" I can't remember her exact response, but I *do* remember feeling like a piece of shit. The duration of the conversation (before she noticed that I was on the verge of tears) made me feel ugly and gross. Finally, when I couldn't take it any more, I managed to mutter, "God, you make me feel bad." She glanced over at me, and when she saw how pathetic I must have looked, she offered some consolation: "Oh, no, no, no...! It doesn't apply to you, because you're not in my family." What a lame thing to say, I thought. Then I responded, "But it does apply to me. You think I'm too dark to be with one of your sons." It took everything I had to hold the tears back or not to get out of the car on the freeway and start walking. After the initial shock, I got pissed and started wishing I had something mean and fucked up to say about her that would hurt her the way she had hurt me. I wanted to scream at her, "I wouldn't wanna date one of your fucked up, stupid ass sons anyway." I began to wonder how I could have been friends with someone who would make me feel so bad, someone so ignorant. In her efforts to console me further, she said that she was just being honest and up front, adding that a lot of people had the same feelings but were just not bold enough to say it. She meant dumb enough.

In essence, she was saying that no matter how nice I am, no matter how bright I am, or that I don't lie, cheat or steal—I am too dark to be in her family. It made me wonder how many other times I had been judged by my complexion. Who knows how many times I had been over-looked or not even considered for something because I'm too dark. I couldn't help but think that if I didn't have a complex about being dark before, I sure as hell would develop one hanging around her. She made me realize that I am not impervious to other people's ignorance.

It's kind of hard to develop a positive self-image as a black person in America when you are constantly being bombarded with images that say: "White (or the closest thing to it) is right." It's no accident that practically every black woman on television, in magazines, in catalogs, and in the movies looks mixed and has long, flowing curly tresses. Black folks have a variety of hair textures, skin colors, and facial features, but you would never know it by images the media portrays. Commercials and ads for cosmetics use models who, if it were not for their color, you wouldn't know were black. And these women are supposed to be representative of black America? In fact, one major cosmetics corporation claims to be "redefining beautiful," using the same old tired models they've always had. Maybe they should pick up a dictionary and use it, because they're not "redefining" jack! Personally, I find it offensive and an insult to my intelligence. It will probably not be in my lifetime that we will finally see images of black women as we really are: African facial features, various hair textures, body types, and all.

Black people have always had big, excuse me, "full" lips, but somehow it didn't become a sign of "beauty" until they made it so. Images of beauty from fashion magazines made a strong impression on me as a teenager growing up in northern

California. Consequently I grew up hating my nose, wishing it wasn't so round. I didn't go so far as to walk around with a clothes pin on my nose to make it smaller and pointier like the character in one of Gloria Naylor's books, but I remember not being thrilled about the one I have. I used to say that if I could ever afford it, I would get a nose job. I never considered that hating my nose was a feeling of self-hatred, nor did I understand why I hated it. It's funny to think that lately I have been thinking about getting my nose pierced. A true sign of personal growth perhaps, thinking about drawing attention to the very thing that I hated and wished to change while growing up. I guess I've become what some would call a "proud jigaboo." Having short hair made me pay more attention to my features and actually appreciate my face. We black women need to learn how to put ourselves on pedestals. Sitting around waiting for white America (or most black men) to do it is something that might never happen.

L̲earning to understand the effect of media on us and analyzing popular culture have both contributed to my growth and development. I still get disgusted, but I just limit the amount of exposure I have to television, magazines and cranked-out, formula Hollywood movies. It helps, but

I think as long as I live in a society where the dominant culture is white, I will always have these things to deal with.

One undiscrimating day, I saw a black man on *Love Connection* say (on national television, mind you) that he wished he looked more like Tom Cruise. This threw me for a loop. It made me realize that these issues of beauty and self-image do not affect only women and children.

As a teenager I was completely sprung on Prince and was convinced that we were cosmically connected since our birthdays were only two days apart. I came to realize how color struck Prince is and wondered how I could have been head over heels for someone who probably wouldn't give the likes of me the time of day. The same thing with Michael Jackson, only "light skin and long hair" weren't good enough for him. He goes for the real thing: ofays. Aside from Diana "the weave queen" Ross, you never heard of or saw him with a black woman. It was always Tatum O'Neal, Liz Taylor, or Brooke Sheilds—and now it's Lisa Marie Presley! Can you imagine the effect that had on the egos of susceptible black girls across the country? He's telling them "it doesn't matter if you're black or white," yet he's doing everything in his power not to look black. It's quite a destructive message.

In another incidence, Lisa Bonet, in a *Rolling Stone* magazine interview said that she doesn't consider herself a black woman. Imagine that! If she doesn't consider herself a black woman then why did she audition for a role on a television show about a black family, and how did she wind up on the cover of a black women's magazine? They're not in the habit of putting ofays on the cover of *Essence* magazine.

And what about Whoopi Goldberg, who—when asked about her ancestry—started talking about her German, French, and Irish blood and didn't once mention African, which obviously

should have been the first thing out of her mouth. I'm not trying to "dis" these people; I'm just using them as examples and
as possible answers to a question that I have yet to figure out...

what is so God-awful about
being just black, plain ole black?

I understand that in show business, people with a certain
"look" are the ones who work and are sometimes considered
better suited for the role. A casting director, I read somewhere,
told a black actress that she was too dark for a role she had
auditioned for. She cried for weeks after that. I've heard countless other horror stories from my own friends in "the business,"
and thanks to them, any thoughts, hopes, or dreams I may have
had about being in show biz were completely released. I am
constantly amazed and angered by the things they tell me
they're subjected to as black women trying to get work in an
industry dominated and run by white men whose perception of
"beauty" for people of color is racist and biased. What it boils
down to is that no matter how much talent you have or where
you went to school, whether or not you work depends on how
close you are to the white ideal.

Being a "regular-looking" black person (as my friends are) is
not an advantage, in fact, it's more likely a disadvantage. It
seems to me that having one white parent has become a prereq-
uisite for black women working in the entertainment industry. I
have so much more respect for people in that business who stick
to their guns about their appearance and define their "look" for
themselves. Personally, I couldn't have someone telling me
directly, in so many words, that I'm too ugly for the job. I'll

stick to the subliminal method. Thank you, very much.

My grandmother on my fathers' side looks like she could be a full-blooded Native American, but I never remember hearing her describe herself as anything other than "just black." I have pictures of her when she was young, and she was absolutely gorgeous (as far as I am concerned, still is). If anybody could claim to be "mixed" with something, she could but choses not to and in raising her children, didn't instill this kind of attitude in them. How she managed to come to this being born in Louisiana, where skin color is as much an issue as race, is beyond me. She's funny because she has long hair, but that's not one of her issues either. She has been known to cut her hair from the middle of her back to just above her ears, in a heart beat. "It ain't nothin' but hair," she says. "It grows back."

This is damn near the year two thousand, and we pretend like this stuff went out the window when black people were wearing afros and screaming, "I'm black and I'm proud." But I'm here to tell you that, unfortunately, the window must have been closed, because these issues are *still* very much a part of the black community.

Things may have gotten a little better—we don't have the "paper bag" test now, and there are fewer offensive ads for beauty products for us jigaboos, but I think it's up to the individual to come to terms with what it means to be "beautiful." I'd just like for it to be known—not just when it comes to blacks but for people of color in general—

> *that there is no one "type" of beauty, and that "type" is not neccesarily the next best thing to white.*

places

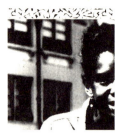

educational
theatre

I am a college graduate. I have earned an undergraduate degree from what is arguably the finest public university in the United States, the University of California at Berkeley. This accomplishment doesn't feel like much to me, but the irony I find utterly fascinating. According to America's educational system, I was not college material and therefore not encouraged to pursue a college education. The correct term for this is "tracking," a process by which students are geared toward a particular course curriculum. Somehow my advisors and counselors never encouraged me to take the necessary courses to attend college; they never even asked me if I *wanted* to attend college! Not once was the college entrance exam mentioned to me. Fortunately, I had family and friends who knew my potential and encouraged me to go to college anyway. I went to a junior college, made the honor roll my first year and transferred to Cal in exactly two years—as I had planned.

Growing up I'd changed schools about every two years. All the way from pre-school through my undergraduate education I bounced around from school to school, and with the exception of about four years, I received my entire education in predominantly white institutions, which is strange since I have always lived in black neighborhoods. Where you attend school can have a great impact on your character, personality, and the kind of person you will become, I think. My first two years of school (pre-school and kindergarten) were at Longfellow Elementary, only a block from where I live now. I spent the fifth and sixth grades at Golden Gate Elementary, which is in my current neighborhood as well. I had black female teachers who took a particular interest in me.

In kindergarten, I had a teacher named Mrs. Hamilton. She was my first "real" teacher. Talk about *Twilight Zone* ! I ran into her at my college graduation. I hadn't seen her in sixteen years, and she remembered me, and I remembered her. I must have been the teacher's pet in kindergarten class, because I remember spending the weekend at her house. She was a young woman with no children, and since I've always been a well-mannered, engaging child, I guess I appealed to her maternal instincts. At five years old, I was easy bait, so I got beat up a lot and often came home with my hair messed up. Family or close friends had to force me to fight my battles. My most memorable experience about my childhood was the day I went to school wearing new shoes and somehow got talked into trading shoes for the day. I actually came home with someone else's old shoes on. That's the kind of child I was.

places...educational theatre

For the fifth and sixth grades I had a teacher named Ms. Moy. She was a beautiful black woman from the south. Georgia, I believe. She was very confident and very feminine at the same time. And she didn't take no mess. She even had the class clowns in line. It felt like we were her children instead of her students; she talked to us and treated us that way. I remember feeling that it really mattered to her that we learned. It had to, nobody would be that tough for nothing. Well, she saw through me like a piece of glass. I always did just enough to get by, and she called me on it. I always found myself in front of the class at the blackboard working on a math problem. I tried to be inconspicuous and hide, but she busted me all the time. She often told me that I didn't need to cheat myself, that I had a lot of potential. She would encourage me to write and often complimented me on my stories. I received a thank you letter from some construction workers and, instead of just giving it to me, Ms. Moy read it out loud to the class. I was always shy and remember feeling like I was about an inch tall:

As a member of the preventative maintenance team that was on the site of Golden Gate School this last week, I wish to express my personal appreciation as well as that of my team mates to one Aliona Gibson. This young lady is the first in sixteen schools to extend her gratitude for our endeavors. Granted we were here to accomplish our specific duties, but whether or not she was prompted to extend us this courtesy is of no consequence. We remain deeply touched.

Those were the only years I spent at mostly black'schools. For first and second grades, I went to a Catholic school, which means that I should know who Pontius Pilate was, but I guess I was too young or just forgot about him. At Golden Gate Public School, I met my first best friend in the whole world, Detra Woodard. We hung around each other so much that we started to look like each other. She got a scholarship to a college prep high school—and I went to Albany—so we drifted apart. Interestingly enough, we wound up in college at Berkeley together years later.

My first year of junior high school was the first time I had ever been to Albany, a small city so close to but so different from Oakland. Before going to Albany Middle School I had never before been around so many white people for any extended period. In their efforts to get me the "best possible public education," my parents discovered this quaint, hick town for me to attend school. I was in my first year of school there when President Reagan was shot. You would have thought he was dead the way everybody at the school was acting. The school administrators were crying and carrying on. It was a strange contrast, because in my neighborhood people were like, "They didn't kill his old ass?"

Coming from Golden Gate, Albany was a complete change for me. I met and made friends with people of races I had only heard about and others I had never known existed. I had a crush on a Korean boy named Jim Kim. He liked me too, but we just flirted and teased each other. Back then I never would have admitted to having a crush on him. Mateo Romero was a Native

American I didn't understand at the time. He was really quiet and basically kept to himself. He was quick to put those white kids in line if they messed with him. They knew that, so nobody did. Pauline Hurtado, a low-rider Chicana, was the coolest thing around. For some strange reason she took a liking to me, and we became fast friends. Before I met Nadir, a boy from Iran, I had no idea where that place was. I probably had never even heard of it, and I know for a fact that I had never heard of Laos. Going to school outside of Oakland and the black community, being exposed to kids from so many different places, was the best thing about going to school in Albany. All of these friends from different places were in addition to my black friends of course, and I never purposely excluded myself from blacks the way some of the other black kids did.

In the seventh grade, still at Albany Middle School, I went on a field trip that introduced me to a whole new world, a week-long trip to Yosemite National Park. I had never been away from home before (for longer than overnight), I had never been camping before, nor did I have any appreciation for natural settings. This field trip is responsible for my love of nature. We were required to go on nature hikes, one of which included a hike up the side of one of the many famous water falls of the park. How beautiful the whole place seemed, the water a green mist mirroring the plants behind it. This was Vernal Falls. If I remember correctly, I was concerned even then with getting my hair wet. I fell in love with Yosemite and learned to pay closer attention to the natural surroundings of the city in which I lived. When we left I swore that I would return to Yosemite one day.

Going to a predominately white school changed my personality a little. I remember my taste in music being "slightly" altered and not being able to figure out why I didn't have the same "rhythm" I once had. I grew to like white rock groups that I had never listened to before, and family and friends would comment about how and why I liked "that noise." It trips me out to think that I used to jam to songs by groups called The Cure or the Talking Heads or Frankie Goes to Hollywood—I hear their songs now, and I am not moved. They merely remind me of my junior high and high school days. I was really into David Bowie and The Rolling Stones in those days. I never got into acid rock, heavy metal, or country music; I liked modern rock in addition to whatever black music was popular at the time. I remember learning "Rappers Delight" and knew it like the back of my hand. I couldn't quite comprehend mitosis and meiosis or photosynthesis, but I could sing "Rappers Delight" at the drop of a hat. I drooled over the models in *G.Q.* magazine and thought the most popular white boys in the school were totally gorgeous. I saw one of those white boys a couple of years after we graduated and thought he was gross. That I could ever have thought he was cute! I even paid money to see that movie *Fast Times at Ridgemont High*. In retrospect, I'm so happy I lived around black people when I was going to school in Albany. If I hadn't, I'd probably have been like some of those black kids that I've met—if you couldn't see them, you wouldn't have known they were black. I don't mean to sound like you have to be a certain way to be black. I, more than anybody, should know that being "black" doesn't mean acting in a stereotypical manner. I'm talking about not having any ties or any dealings with other black people, by choice.

I had a friend who made it known that she didn't like black boys. She only liked white, Mexican, or Filipino boys. If she went out with a black boy, he had to be half-white, or look half-white. Just as I had never been to Albany before junior high school, most of the kids I was friendly with had probably never been to Oakland. I can't imagine growing up without other black people around.

> *The important thing to remember when raising black children in a predominately white environment is to make sure they maintain a strong identity and a positive self-image.*

My sense of style and the clothes I wore also reflected the kind of environment I was in at the time. At one point, without really acknowledging it, the "look" I was trying to achieve was that of a middle-class white girl from the suburbs. I was really into the preppie look and somehow managed to have clothes designed by Ralph Lauren and Izod LaCoste. I didn't have every color or every designer shirt like some of the other kids, but I did own enough colors to wear the layered look, which consisted of a polo shirt underneath a long-sleeved, button-down oxford shirt. I capped that off with a wool Ralph Lauren cardigan sweater, which I proudly wore with the little polo emblem. To this I added a pair of Sperry Topsiders or penny loafers. Dressing preppy is easy. It takes no sense of style, no creativity, no individuality. Designer clothes were a status symbol and were worn by the most popular and coolest kids in the school. I remember being ecstatic when I got a pair of Jordache jeans. For a brief period in about the tenth grade I went through a mild punk rock stage. I just wore off-the-wall, weird stuff I wasn't used to and topped it off with an old denim jacket from the sixties that my mother used to wear. I covered the jacket with a bunch of Prince pins and buttons. That's as far as I got into the punk rock look.

It was during this period that I had to be forced to wear normal clothes, which to me was anything other than jeans and a t-shirt, to see the play *Dreamgirls*. I actually thought I could go to see a Broadway play in a pair of jeans. Of course, my parents weren't having it. There's a picture of me on that night, and I actually had an attitude and was pouting. I had learned how to taper jeans to make them straight legged and used the sewing machine I got for Christmas to taper the legs of every single pair of jeans I owned. I guess I was pseudo-punk rock; the real punk rockers were kids who cut their hair into a mohawk and dyed it red or green (or hydrogen peroxied it if they were black). They wore black leather, chains, and spikes and had six or seven piercings, in one ear. *I* even thought they were weird, especially the black kids who got into the punk rock/skin head look. When I asked my mother if I could get a second hole in one of my ears, she said no. I remember thinking that's what you get for asking.

After my brief period on the wild side I became bored with the preppie look, and I guess I thought I needed to change my image since I would be going to high school. From one of the teen magazines I used to buy, I discovered Esprit de Corps. When I found out the outlet was in San Francisco, my mother and I rushed over and got on the mailing list. Pretty soon, practically everything I owned was made by Esprit de Corp. I got postcards about their huge sales, and we would go wait in line with a bunch of other mothers and daughters, mostly white, from all over the Bay Area. My mother has always liked nice clothes. She always shopped at Macy's, Emporium and I. Magnin for clothes for my brother and me. I loved the Esprit style—it was less rigid and conservative than the preppie look. Now that I think about it, it was probably less "white-looking" too. I think what initially attracted me to Esprit was the fact that they used people of color in their ads. Without paying it any real attention, I suppose I felt more connected with the company image. They used black girls who looked like me in their ads.

> *You couldn't pay me to wear anything by Ralph Lauren now. Aside from being ridiculously over-priced, I can't stand the lily-white, pure, all-American image the company projects.*

Junior high and high school were the times in my life when I cared the most about clothes. After that, shopping and dressing never became a serious pre-occupation of mine. That might be attributed to growing up in California, and being at Berkeley didn't help. My friend Tonya and I tripped when she called me from Howard University her first semester and told me in amazement how much people were into clothes and dressing.

They actually got dressed up to sit in classes all day! I really tripped when she said they change clothes for dinner. I considered Tonya a good dresser, so I figured if *she* was bugging. I would definitely be out of my element at Howard. In college I got into what some people would call the bummy look. Of course, I didn't think it was bummy at all since everything I wore was always clean. It was casual and comfortable, which was becoming more and more of a priority with me. I only wore jeans, sweat pants, t-shirts and sweat shirts. By the time I got to Cal, wearing what was comfortable enough to hang out on the grass while I cut class was my only concern. My boyfriend at the time hated my sweats and threatened to throw them away. He'd tease, saying he would never have to worry about losing me to a Nigerian, because they simply would not have me, not dressed like that.

As an adult, I've grown to accept the fact that I'm just not a stylish or trendy person. Between being a native Californian and spending time in Berzerkeley, dressing to impress just hasn't become a priority in my life. I try to look at it in a positive light: I have my own style. I am no longer ruled by peer pressure or the need to be one of the "in" people, so I just buy what I like and, more importantly, what's on sale. This means I usually end up with a bunch of clothes that don't match, style-wise. So as a person who gets an instant headache from places like the Nordstrom Rack or Filene's Basement, I decided a while ago that whenever I see something that grabs me, I should just get it, sometimes regardless of the price.

I sort of lost touch with the fact that I'm a fashion misfit until one time my friend Shiree was talking to our friend Alison on the phone, and I was told she said, "Oh, my God, Alison, you have to see Aliona. She's matching today." My feelings were hurt at first, then I got a serious attitude. I said to myself: She has her damn nerve, trying to cap on somebody. Every other time we go out together we look like the damn Bobsey twins. Now I am such an individualist that it annoys the hell out of me when I think I look like everyone else. Most of the time I don't, as reigning fashion misfit. Since college I've thought that clothes and dressing were shallow and superficial shit anyway.

> *There's more to me than what's*
> *on the outside; it's really about*
> *what kind of person you are.*

In the tenth grade I got a D+ in a typing class and lost my out-of-district permit to attend Albany High, so I went to Berkeley High, which was my introduction to the world of drugs and alcohol. Fortunately for me, I've always been a chicken, so I never got around to the serious drugs. However, I *did* drink my share of forty ouncers of "eight ball" and Bacardi 151 rum. The closest I ever came to trying anything stronger was when I was at a frat party and somebody offered me a few lines. I had heard about cocaine and knew people who did it, but I was too scared to try it. I've always been afraid of having a bad trip or getting too high and staying that way. I was already drunk off a forty of Old E, so I agreed to do the lines. Fuck it, I thought. Might as well find out what all the fuss is about. But when I returned from walking one of my drunk friends to her car, the coke person was gone.

I didn't realize how much of a "wild child" I had become until I ran into the mother of one of my hanging buddies. When I told her that I had just graduated from college, she said, "College? Graduated? You? I didn't think you were the college type." Needless to say, I pondered the kind of impression I had given this woman.

The only high school in a "racially diverse" city, Berkeley High had students from all over the world and a lot of racially mixed kids. For the most part, the blacks hung out in one area and the whites in another. I hung out somewhere in the middle with the folks who didn't want to be restricted to one group. There must have been six of us young women, three white and three black, that traveled in a pack. We were all very close and did everything together. It's O.K. to have white friends, but it becomes a problem when, as a black person, they are your *only* friends. It was not uncommon to see black kids who hung out exclusively with whites; somehow it validated them, making them feel more important. Hanging out with my white girlfriends didn't make me feel any more important or popular, and I wasn't friends with them just because they were white. We were the Berkeley High "rainbow coalition." Unlike in high school, my interaction with white people is very limited these days. I don't feel like I have enough in common with any white woman to develop a close friendship. This was a totally foreign concept to me when I was in school.

I went to class at Berkeley High, but I partied up at Cal with the college crowd. Even though the frat houses were all white and very few of the guys were twenty-one, they had hella wild parties with ten and twelve kegs of beer, plus hard alcohol for the serious drinkers. It's amazing that I'm still alive to tell these stories. Like many other teenagers at the time, we were completely oblivious to Mothers Against Drunk Drivers and the "Don't Do Drugs" propaganda. I had no idea how much I was putting my life on the line. There were several occasions when I actually could have been killed. Like the time I drove down from the Berkeley Hills at night, on a two-lane road overlooking the whole Bay Area, in a van sitting sideways on this guy's lap. He was operating the pedals, and I was steering and trying to look at the view at the same time. I went to the parties of what I considered to be "rich" white kids in the Berkeley Hills. When someone's parents went out of town, the house would be used for a huge, all-night party. Naturally, there were mostly white people, but it never bothered me, because I was never the only black person in the room. Even if I had been, it wouldn't have bothered me nearly as much as it would now. In fact, I probably wouldn't have even noticed with my rose tints on. Plus, at Berkeley High, a "multi-cultural Mecca," to have black friends made you in vogue, in style. At the other schools I went to (Albany, Diablo Valley College, and Cal), the blonde-hair, blue-eyed girls were the standard of beauty; at Berkeley High being "mixed" was the in thing.

I noticed that the kids who were bi-racial usually identified with the white folks and were the most sought after. That's not just at Berkeley High, I think that's a Bay Area thang. Whiteness is such a part of the culture that if you're not that, the next best thing is just as good. It was a learning experience, but I don't think that

I would have gotten any less of an education had I gone to school in Oakland.

In my last semester of college, I got an F in my African history class. My professor said that my attendance was not indicative of someone interested in learning about the history of Africa. I was cutting the class to work on my thesis, which I had waited until the last minute to do. I fell three units short of the necessary to get my degree. Ordinarily, I would have gone to summer school to make up the course and get the degree. Since I had made plans to leave the Bay Area and later the state, it would be two-and-a-half years later that I made up the class and actually got the piece of paper. In that two-year period, nobody ever asked to see my degree, and I never offered.

For all of those people who think we don't have "overt racism" in California: During the time I attended junior college, a black man was hanged from a tree near the same B.A.R.T. station where I got off every day. The incident was a definite cover up and was racially motivated since, oddly enough, the northern California Ku Klux Klan headquarters was located in the same town. My point in mentioning this is to give you an idea of the kind of city Pleasant Hill is. I saw it as a kind of a time warp. There were white people walking around with bell bottom jeans and feathered haircuts. It was like Albany, but a lot worse and on a much larger scale. Even though it was only a forty-five minute train ride and on the other side of the mountains, it seemed like it was somewhere in the deep South, Tennessee or Alabama maybe.

I never experienced any blatant racism myself, but you can feel when tension is in the air or when you're being watched. It was a country town where it was not uncommon to see a pick-up truck with a shot-gun in the back window. O.K., maybe that could be innocuous, but you get my drift. Since I had gone to high school in Albany, I was used to this kind of environment, plus, by this time I was so focused and directed that I knew what I was there for, and that was my sole objective.

Most of my friends were women, and I maintained my association with some of the fellas from Berkeley High who had also made the trek across the mountains. They were there to more or less check out the "Contra Costa County babes" (ofays). I got to Diablo Valley College with a game plan and went to work. My grades there were the best of my entire scholastic career, which made me feel pretty good since this was supposed to be such a "good" school. My only real concern was making sure I was on the train heading to Oakland before dark—I never forgot that lynching. I made it my job to educate these poor, uninformed classmates by giving a lecture on apartheid in South Africa for my speech class. I remember being amazed by how little they knew. At the height of the South African political activity in the Bay Area, these people hadn't a clue. I went all out and made copies of a Brenda Payton column that provided a list of all the American corporations doing business in South Africa and gave out red ribbons to wear in support of the struggle in South Africa. I remember taking a dance class and feeling like I was Judith Jamison—powerful. There were no other black people in this town! But, thanks to my prior schooling, it was nothing I had not already experienced. My social interaction with other students was very minimal, and for the first time since junior high school, I had practically no white friends, and I didn't mind.

At Cal Berkeley, all of my friends during my first semester were Asian. It wasn't until the semester before my last, when I lived in the dorm, that I began to meet other black people. The black student population at Cal was very small. You'd think that a special effort would be made to have a better support system, especially since we were dropping out like flys. Because I was not into the Greek way of life (you know, Q-dogs, AKA, A phi A), the black students ignored me. I just could not get with that Greek mess. I'll never understand why anybody has to be part of an elite group to serve the community or do all of the other good things that they want to do. I see it as being another way in which we try to emulate white people. I think fraternities and sororities are very class-oriented, and I've never felt like I needed to "belong" to a social organization to get things done, especially one that uses physically harming and demeaning tactics for initiation. So, until I met black folks who had the same attitude, I hung out by myself or with the people I met through my classes.

I was an English major my first semester at Cal; that's exactly how long that brilliant idea lasted—one semester. I had a particularly rough time at Cal at first. For a minute, I actually hated it and thought about dropping out until I became aware of the retention rate of black students there and realized that that's exactly what I was expected to do, give up.

If I *had* dropped out, there was something else I needed to take into consideration—whether or not I wanted to continue living. Joy would have killed me. She was another one of the *Essence* women who took me under her wing. I wasn't too concerned with the lecture I'd have to endure from my parents. I was more concerned about dealing with Joy. She made it clear that she wasn't helping me out for her health. Speaking on behalf of Paulette and Elaine, two other mentors, she told me if I expected to get anywhere in life, school (not necessarily college), was unavoidable.

*She told me that in our society
I already had two strikes
against me,
being black and
being female,
and that regardless of what
I wanted to do, a college
education would not be a
disadvantage.*

Apart from all that, she had spent hundreds of dollars on my school books, and if I thought I was just going to drop out and throw her money away, I had another thing coming. My three friends made me feel like I needed to just go ahead and "knock it out." They convinced me that it would be wiser (and easier) to do it at twenty instead of doing it at forty.

That thought brought to mind Elaine Minor, a family friend. She was in her late thirties and a junior in college after taking a twenty-year hiatus to get married and raise a family. She lived in the dormitory and was totally involved in campus activities. I admired her for her vigor and assurance as an undergraduate. Elaine was older than my mother, but had an energy level of which I could only dream. I often wondered why I wasn't having as much fun as she seemed to be having. We ended up graduating the same year. She was forty-one, going to law school and everything. At twenty-one, I knew that I, under any circumstances, would not want to be in school (of all places) in twenty years, so I managed to stick it out, barely.

College was hard for me, and I really felt like they didn't care whether or not you passed your classes--or even if you went to class--as long as you paid your tuition. Had I attended a smaller college, I might have gotten a better education. A black college would have been ideal. Somehow I think at a black college your best interest is taken to heart, and the professors really do care whether or not you learn and pass your courses. Even if that's not the case, going to a school where professors, not just those in the African-American studies department, are black has to have positive impact on black students. Coming from this region of the country, just going to a black school period can be a profound experience. Growing up in predominantly white environments, which is not a hard thing to do in California, can make for very confused and misguided children who, if they don't get a serious reality check, will grow up to be very confused and misguided adults. My reality check was the fact that I lived in Oakland, with black folks, thank God.

> *It scares me to think what I might have been if I had gone to school in mostly white areas and lived there too!*

At Cal I took an Asian-American studies class in which I was the only black person and the only non-Asian person in the class. I learned that they have some of the same problems and concerns that we have in the black community and realized that there are some definite cultural similarities between us. On the Cal campus there were a lot of interracial couples among the Asian students as well, which caused problems in their campus community. A lot of the Asian women were dating the white male students, so much that the Asian men felt invisible and obsolete. Black women did the same on campus and, in a much bigger picture, probably throughout the state of California. Cal Berkeley, in the same way as Berkeley High, had a reputation for being a Mecca of "multi-culturalism." Asian women were seen as "exotic" (which as a woman of color, I find personally offensive) and therefore sought after by the white men on campus. One of my male friends on the east coast jokingly said that the black women should hook up with the Asian guys, and then everybody would be happy. (I did not think that was funny.)

> *Cal was my introduction to the term "people of color." It was the first time that I became aware of the fact that some of the things that we have (and do)*

> *experience as black people in this country are not uniquely ours.*

I had Chicana friends who explained to me that their parents didn't want them to speak Spanish or that it was better to bring a white boy home than a black one, and Asians who said that skin color was a major issue in their community as well. Being mixed (with white, of course) is looked upon highly and constitutes what is considered "beautiful" by their standards as well. It was a trip, and I didn't quite understand why it took coming to Cal for me to recognize these things.

Aside from the people I met and the required reading lists from my classes, my senior thesis project was the most rewarding aspect of my two-year stay at Cal. I wrote a paper on American standards of beauty and how they effect women of color. I interviewed women about their experiences, how their ideas of what is beautiful were formed and how they viewed themselves. In my efforts to do research, I found little material on women of color. All of the books I found were about white women and, at the most, had a few chapters on our experiences. I was really disturbed when this was a topic of discussion on the *Geraldo* show, and the panel did not have one woman of color. What qualifies these women to speak on this issue? Unless you know from personal experience, in my opinion, you have *no* business addressing such concerns. I didn't know until the black graduation (a special commencement for the black students) that there were so many black students on campus. I was on my way out before I was introduced to my fellow African-Americans. With a student body of thirty thousand plus I guess it would be kind of hard to connect, but a special effort should have been made toward developing that "connection."

For graduate school, I'm thinking about going to a black college where that "connection" comes effortlessly. I try very hard to encourage young black students here to go to black colleges, or at least to visit one. Coming from out west, it would be a sort of "rite of passage" to go to a black school. I'm glad I went to Cal, but I think getting an education from a historically black college would not have allowed me to slip through the cracks the way I did at Berkeley. Howard University, Spelman, Hampton, Fisk, Tuskeegee, Clark, Atlanta U, Morgan State.... I never thought *I'd* feel this way about school, but now I can hardly wait. I'm sure that it will be quite an experience.

goin' home

When I graduated from high school in 1985, I was in the middle of my obsession with Marilyn Monroe, in love with the group WHAM!, and aching to go to college in La-La land (Los Angeles). Despite all of this, I wouldn't go so far as to say I was a completely white-washed, disillusioned teenager, but I was definitely the product of an experiment; someone uprooted from the black community, subsequently developing uncommon traits and characteristics for an average black child raised in Oakland. I had my little white girl-friends and was probably more concerned with making sure we kept in contact than I was with what I was going to do with the rest of my life. I thought going to Africa would be "interesting" rather than a pilgrimage home or an experience that could change my life. I really had no idea of what was in store. Perhaps such immaturity is to be expected of an eighteen year old.

Before the trip to Africa, I had never been out of California. Imagine that! Your first trip out of the state is half way around the world to the land of your ancestors. Deep. I attended the 1985 International Women's Conference in Kenya. It didn't dawn on me just how intense an experience that would be or how much it would effect my life until after I got back. In all honesty (my code of ethics), I was actually more excited about going to Italy after visiting Kenya and the conference. It's sickening, and I'm almost too embarrassed to share that fact, but it's true. Somewhere in my junior high and early high school years, I developed a fascination for Italian anything: clothes, cars, food, and men. Not Italian-Americans, the "real" Italians. I'd heard about how much they "love" black women and thought: Finally, some men with some damn sense. Needless to say, after a couple of days in Kenya, Italy was the *last* thing on my mind. Thanks to the travel-agent-from-hell our plans to stop in Italy on our way back to the states fell through, and we were able to stay in Mombassa for an extra week. Mombassa, I decided, was absolute paradise. It also happened to be the birthplace of the man I was pursuing, being pursued by, and with whom I would eventually fall in love.

The most evident sign of how profound an experience my trip to Africa was has to be my first-semester grades in college. I will be the first to say that I've always been an average student in school, getting B's was a major accomplishment for me. I settled for C's, and B's made me ecstatic, so when I got four A's and a B my first semester of college, I just about had a cow. I was given a party for this incredible feat. I remember thinking: Damn, I should have gone somewhere every summer, I would have been on the honor roll all through school. It was as though I was on some kind of drug or something, like I was high as the sky...I was feeling *goooood*. I was high on life.

Everything I talked and wrote about had something to do with my trip to Kenya. I could have been having a conversation with someone about the price of tea in China, and somehow I would have brought Kenya into the conversation. I felt energized and had a particular eagerness to share my experiences with other people, sort of reminding myself how lucky I was to have been given such a wonderful high school graduation present. For months I went on and on about my trip. I had a lot of nerve looking at my mom like she was crazy and hoping she would shut up about Egypt and the Nile when she got back from her first trip to Africa. But in my eagerness to share what I had seen with other people, I became disgusted about how miseducated black people were (and are) about Africa.

Even adults (black and white) asked me some of the most ridiculous questions you can imagine: "Where did you sleep?"—as if they could only imagine huts in a jungle. They wanted to know what I ate, and if I saw any starving people when I told them I was near Ethiopia. They wanted to know how "those Africans" treated me (knowing that I am an African American). I found myself having to explain repeatedly that Nairobi is like a small San Francisco that even had a Kentucky Fried Chicken and a Barclays Bank. It was difficult and frustrating to answer the most basic questions, but I had to remember that it was the same miseducation about Africa and our people that had me looking forward to going to Europe more than Africa. I explained so many times that because of colonialism, everybody spoke English and told people that, even to my surprise, there were white people there, not just on vacation, people who actually lived there and had been there for generations and considered themselves Africans. I decided that it was a conspiracy: The whites wanted us to be ignorant about Africa, to hate it, so they could have it all to themselves. It made me sick. They were "living large" and having a ball, in Africa !!!

I began to better understand why black people disassociated themselves from Africa and would fight you for calling them an African.

It was through this single experience that I began to examine the impact of the media on us. I somehow developed "selective amnesia" about what I imagined Africa to be like before I actually went there. Would I be asking another tourist the same dumb-ass questions people were asking me? The answer is probably yes, and that bothered me. I felt so honored and fortunate to have been able to go and see it for myself. I know it sounds corny, but I'm going to say it anyway: I think all African-Americans need to go and see it for themselves; it's not at all like what we've been told.

Our brothers and sisters on the continent needed to be given the 4-1-1 on America as well. I told them that we had people sleeping in the streets and had a particularly rough time trying to convince folks that I was not rich, explaining that both of my parents worked, that we were working class, and that they had to save money for me to be able to visit Africa. In an effort to prove me wrong, I had a young man ask me how many cars my family owned. That, to him, would be an indication of wealth. I fell out laughing and begged him to ask me *anything* else. How could I explain that we had four cars but only one and a half worked; in fact, one of those four was buried in weeds in our backyard.

Just being in Nairobi was a thrill: to see two men in business suits walking down the street holding hands in public (and you know its not a stance of gay affection, because homosexuality is against the law and punishable by death); or to pay three dollars for the same Kenya bag you've seen at Macy's for twenty-five; to meet a man who tells you he has four wives, and that you look like number three; or to have people ask you if you know Lionel Ritchie when you tell them you live in California, having the same Africans, whom you were told hate your guts and think you have a slave mentality, embrace you and welcome you home with open arms. The whole thing was an intense experience—from the malaria shots, the twenty-two hour flight (with an overnight stay in London), and falling head over heels for one of the "natives"—to finally coming back to a welcome home dinner of macaroni and cheese, collard greens and fried chicken.

It was all an experience that undoubtedly changed my perception of the world and my place in it.

No one made me consider that a trip to Africa would be the best thing that could have happened to me and at eighteen would prove to be the most influential experience of my young life. I had gone to "good schools," yet I had been looking forward to going to Rome more than to Nairobi. In retrospect, it was probably the "good" schools that diverted my interests towards someone else's history and culture other than my own. A case of self-hatred and denial or just another miseducated and ill-informed young African American?

To make sure I wasn't "on my own" for the trip, my mother asked Paulette, Melody, and Elaine to keep an eye on me. A month would be the longest I'd ever been away from home, and I'm sure sometime before we left she pulled them aside and had a conversation about me, indicating her concern for my safety and well-being. I wasn't the most street-wise teenager around, and yes, I tended to be a little naïve—but I was no dummy and not nearly as sheltered and reserved as my mother thought. I guess I covered my tracks well, because she didn't know anything about the wild college parties I went to that year.

So three women, only twelve years my senior, became my guardians for the trip. Their job was, basically, to make sure I came back the same innocent, reserved teenager as I left. It would be an interesting arrangement since my three guardians each had no children and were in their early thirties; their inter-action with teenagers was limited. They seemed pretty cool to me, which meant they didn't treat me like a baby, and gave me credit for having a little bit of sense. They spoke to me and treat-ed me like I was one of them. I knew everything would be okay when the stewardess on the British Airways flight offered me an alcoholic beverage and I accepted, waiting for an objection from one of them since I wasn't the legal drinking age. They didn't even look surprised. It was as if they had known about my wild drinking escapades, but I knew they couldn't have since we had just recently met. Not only did we end up going out for drinks during the trip, I went to my first adult nightclub with Paulette and Melody at a place in Nairobi called the Carnivore. I had more fun that night than I'd ever had at frat parties watching crazy white boys get drunk and tear shit up. The club, which was jam packed (to my surprise, on a school night) had a live African highlife band, an open ceiling, and an outdoor patio area. I remember looking up and thinking that I'd never seen the sky so clear before. There were more stars in the sky than I had ever seen, even at Yosemite.

That night I also got a good sense of their personalities and just how seriously they planned to take this whole "guardian" thing. Two minutes after we got into the club, I met a guy. We started talking and decided to go out to the patio to finish our conversation in his broken English and my non-existent Swahili. I went back into the crowded club only to find an hysterical Melody and a much-annoyed, but restrained, Paulette. Damn, I thought, leave their sight for a couple of hours, and they lose their minds. They said they were worried about me and had been looking for me for over an hour. Melody said she got a small cigarette hole burned in the back of her shirt from running through the club like a madwoman looking for me. She went completely off on me, giving me a lecture about how we were in a different country and how dangerous it was to leave with some strange man and how I needed to be more cautious in dealing with people. Of course, I thought she was totally over-reacting; Sudi was a nice guy. Paulette on the other hand was cool. She pulled me over to the side and calmly told me not to ever do that again. "The next time you decide to vacate the premises, be responsible and courteous enough to let us know, please." I could tell she was upset and concerned, but her response was the complete opposite of Melody's. It would be a couple of years before I understood what they were trying to say. Their admonitions reminded me of how I used to get in trouble all the time for not calling home if I were going to be out later than expected.

The whole experience in Kenya helped me to form several of my life goals, among them moving to Africa at some point to live and work. I would also like to become bi-lingual. There are many people in the world who speak at least two languages, some speak three or four. There were folks in Kenya who hadn't graduated from high school, but who were fluent in English, German and Arabic, in addition to their native tongue. Here I was, a citizen of one of the richest countries in the world, sitting amidst multi-lingual Africans, saying "tengo usted." It was truly embarrassing, especially since my high school was one of the few in the country to offer an African language—Swahili—as part of the curriculum. By the time I got to Berkeley High I had been speaking Spanish and decided to stick with it, not knowing that two years later I'd be going to Africa.

In Kenya I learned about history (colonialism), about geography (standing in the waters of the Indian Ocean—before this trip I don't think I would have been able to find it on a map), about the true meaning of the term "the miseducation of the Negro," and more importantly I learned the value of being able to "go." After that trip I firmly believe that in order to get the "real deal," you have to see for yourself. Rely on images the media feeds you, especially when it comes to black folks, and you might not make it. I know from personal experience.

The trip was a high school graduation gift. I could have had a car, but took the trip instead. Well, it's eight years later, and I still don't have a car, but I *do* still have the memories of my life-changing trip to the land of my ancestors. I have a ton of slides and photographs, a journal that I kept during the trip, and a host of friends I met there. I was more proud to be of African decent after my trip than ever before. If given the choice again, I would choose another trip to Africa over a car any day of the year.

> *It's not about being rich or even
> middle class (of which I am
> neither); it's about priorities.*

It still amazes me that I took a trip at eighteen that a lot of people haven't taken as adults. I feel obligated and honored to share what I have learned with people less fortunate than myself. I think I will always be open to the opportunity to explore new places, new people, and new experiences.

east vs. west

Before traveling internationally, I don't think I gave much thought to traveling inside this country, much less abroad. After Kenya I got a travel bug I am still trying to shake. There were men in other parts of the world who actually found me attractive, so I was ready to go! I knew when I returned that if I didn't make it out of California for college, it would be shortly thereafter.

After my trip to the motherland, I considered myself somewhat a "woman of the world," until I got to New York City.

The east and west coast are like night and day.

I had made up my mind and decided to get the hell out of Dodge after graduating; I was going to be on the first thing heading east. I would be visiting the east coast for the first time during a spring break. It was that first trip to Washington D.C. that convinced me. A high school friend who was at Howard University had invited me to come out for a visit. The idea of an all-black college amazed me, because here in California, a "black" anything often means half the people are white. They are everywhere. You have to search for the black folks in northern California. Oakland is probably the only city in the country where you can go into a black-owned, soulfood restaurant and be the only black person there: Mexicans in the kitchen cooking grits and eggs, white waitresses with a European hostess, who is, of course, married to the owner.

I can't speak on D.C., but in New York there are areas where you can go for days without seeing a white person. I had heard that D.C. was "Chocolate City," and I couldn't wait to see for myself. It was during this visit to D.C. that I was also introduced to the kind of reputation that black people in California have. My first night there I walked into a dorm room in Meridian Hall and caught the tail end of a conversation between a group of female students. They were talking about the Olympic figure skater Debbie Thomas' marriage. "Girl, you know those sisters in California are into white boys." They didn't know I was visiting from California so naturally I had to intervene. I waved my hand and shyly announced that I was from California and was not "into white boys." Though they were clearly embarrassed, they all burst into laughter. It really tripped me out to hear what other people thought about us California black folks.

*I think where you grow up has
a tremendous effect on how you
see things.*

In a lot of ways your environment shapes the kind of person you
are or will become. Obviously, there are both good and bad
things about this. Someone once told me that she thought kids
raised in California saw the world through rose-tinted glasses. I
totally agree. Not just black kids. Kids, in general, have this
romanticized, distorted view of what the world and the people
in it are like. This is probably a result of being so close to
Hollywood, I don't know. For black Californians, it means you
grow up thinking that people are people, that color doesn't matter, and that deep down we're all the same. Having such näive
ideas about what the world is like sets you up for a very rude
awakening, an awakening that reveals, after you get out into the
world and realize that no matter where you went to college or
how articulate you are...

*you are still seen as just
another nigger to some people.*

I realized how internalized and detrimental such thinking can be
when I argued with an old school mate (a black male) from high
school that you don't have to be "doing" anything for the police
to fuck with you: being black and being a man is enough for
them to take the liberty of kickin' your ass. I tried to convince
him that no matter what Rodney King did, he did not deserve
what he got. The Rodney King incident was on tape, I told him,
but that shit happens all the time, and there's nobody around to
catch it. And just because it never happened to him didn't mean

that it didn't ever happen or that it wouldn't happen to him. I couldn't believe he thought otherwise. The whole conversation reminded me of someone I met in New York who accused me of being soft, because I don't rant and rave like a lunatic. I'll be the first to admit that I'm rather low key, but I'm nowhere near comatose like a lot of other people from California.

People with "rose-tints" sit around talking a good game and being all liberal and multicultural, until their daughter brings a black man home. A couple of years after I moved away and came back, I ran into one of my hanging buddies from high school, and in giving me the scoop on the rest of the gang, I learned that the blonde-haired girl with rhythm was not on speaking terms with her parents, because she was living with and engaged to a black man. Of course, this tripped me out: I had met her parents on several occasions, and they didn't seem to have a problem with me or her hanging with us. The whole thing reminded me of something that would have been going on thirty years ago in the deep South somewhere, not in the "liberal" Bay Area.

The west coast stands as a good, solid argument *for* segregation; the black people out here try so hard to be integrated and "accepted" that it makes them weird. It's really integrated, and sometimes that can be a good thing, in terms of making you more tolerant and exposed to different people and different cultures. But in my opinion, integration has it's negative effects as well.

*A lot of people raised in
integrated areas are often
confused and uncertain about
their identity.*

Plus, there's a different breed of white people out here, which accounts for the strange vibe and relationship between blacks and whites. They buy mudcloth or wear African earrings and think that makes them "down for the cause." And a lot of the white people on the west coast are totally patronizing. I'd like to believe that the ones who made friends with me were doing so because of the wonderful and interesting person I am and not because of some guilt trip they're on. It's mostly in California that you see a bunch of white people wearing dreadlocks petitioning for retribution for black people in America. Yes, there is an organization that is actually working toward getting black people "back wages" for the pain and suffering of slavery in this country! I'm all for *that* (as I am always talking about how I never got my forty acres and a mule), but to have white people volunteering their time and energy for something that is as likely as hell freezing over is a bit strange. The kind of strange that can only be found in northern California—they're on a totally different trip in southern California.

Before I went to Africa and found out how empowering it is to be in the majority and developed something of an intolerance for being around whites *all* the time, I wanted to go school in Los Angeles or San Diego. Southern California is worse than the Bay Area in terms of locating black folks and being constantly surrounded by whites, since "finding" the black folks in

California can be pretty hard when we make up less than four percent of the population. So you mix guilty white people with some fun, ofay-loving black folks, and you have an interesting scene. Add a dash of whiteness as the dominant culture, and you get Latinas who hydrogen peroxide their hair, wear blue contacts, and swear they're not trying to be white, or Asian women who have a preference for white boys. Blacks are not the only people of color who love them some white people in California.

On the east coast, the relationship between blacks and whites is totally different. Blacks in the East aren't necessarily trying to be part of the "rainbow coalition," which in my opinion makes for a much stronger black community, and for black people who are comfortable with and confident about their blackness. To be mixed or light-skinned isn't seen as an so much an advantage amongst black people back east as it is in California, it's not a bad thing to consider yourself an African. New York seemed very much like California because of all the different ethnic groups living there. Only I found New York to be much more segregated than California. I was introduced to the "culture of the islands" in Brooklyn, which has the second largest West Indian population outside of the Caribbean. Before living in Spanish Harlem I had never seen any one from Puerto Rico before and probably would not have been able to point the island out on a map. As an African American I was in the minority in my neighborhood. My exposure to and knowledge of Jewish culture was non-existent before New York. I remember the first time I saw an Hassidic Jew, I nearly died of fear. I had never seen one before (to my knowledge), and somehow I had associated their look with some character straight out of the movies.

"White is right" in California, where you have mixed people who consider themselves white and would check white or "neither" if asked to identify their race on a survey. I found black people in the east to be much more black-identified. Even the white people identify with ethnicity more: whites are either Jewish, Polish, Italian, etc. In California, everybody is trying to be the blonde-haired, blue-eyed WASP, even the Asians. This fringe relationship between blacks and whites back east probably has a lot to do with why there are not as many interracial couples there. I've gotten to the point where I almost *expect* a black man to be (or have been) with an ofay.

My introduction to "life on the east coast" was a rally for Yusef Hawkins, a young black man who was in Bensonhurst looking to buy a used car. Bensonhurst is a redneck section of Brooklyn. He was shot and killed by some Italians, because they thought he was looking at or dating some white girl. This scenario would not make it in California. With all the brothers into white girls, it would be a constant mob scene. It's a sad but definite reality. I consider myself a rarity, because I was born and raised in this madness, and I have never been involved with a white man. I definitely wasn't getting action from the brothers, but some of us just choose to do without.

The strong black community in New York makes for a stronger black business community. Black people have and support black businesses there (compared with California). The black folks are self-supporting. To see black businesses doing really well the way they are in New York was totally amazing to me. In Harlem, which was a sight for sore eyes, you can probably buy life insurance on the streets. The "do for self" mentality is not rhetoric in New York City. I witnessed folks doing their own thing, in a serious way. The 125th Street Mart was an awesome scene, and I had never seen anything like it before—over one hundred black-owned businesses all under the same roof. When I came back from living in New York, I had to re-adjust to seeing the majority of street merchants and vendors on Telegraph Avenue and the flea market, where white people wearing red, green, and gold and nose rings try to sell me reggae memorabilia. On 125th and Lenox, it was like an African market place.

The number of natural hair care salons in New York is another example of the difference between the east and west coasts. In the Bay Area we have one well-known salon and maybe a few others that I don't know about, but in NYC there are way more, because there is a huge market for it there. I didn't feel like an alien with a short natural in New York the way I do in California. I walk past black men on the Oakland streets who have shoulder length, permed hair (usually finger waves, Shirley Temple curls, or a Jheri Curl), and they look at *me* like *I'm* crazy. I don't know why I'm always so surprised; we have black people out here who dye their hair honey blonde and think they are too fine. I didn't see any men with processed hair during my two-year stay in New York. I noticed a lot more people with natural hair styles. Dreadlocks were as common as braids. Every and anybody had dreads in New York, people with jobs. Outside of the "cultural crowd" in California, dreads are really trendy. Before they became in vogue, it was mostly homeless people who wore them, not even dreaded but matted with lint and trash in it. There do be a difference.

My friend Michael had never met anybody from the west coast before. I can't wait for him to come to California because he's going to bug *so* hard. I know because he trips off *me*. He thinks I act like a white girl, just like the women I worked with in New York thought. Only they left me alone and made me an official "round-the-way-girl" after they met the quintessential "valley girl" dipped in chocolate from Encino. I'm nowhere near a valley girl, though the people I came into contact with on the east coast thought I was "different" or, as Michael puts it, "weird but in a good way."

My first week in New York on the subway this young brother told me that he knew I was from somewhere else because I talked "white." Naturally I had to go off on him: I told him that obviously he had never been anywhere, because if he had he would have known that people from different places speak differently. Okay no, I don't have a New York accent, but where I come from, how I talk is not "white"; it's the way everybody talks. His comment, however, struck a chord in me. I get so tired of people expecting me to act or talk a certain way because I'm black, and if I don't act that way then I'm trying to be something else or I'm not "down" (for the cause). Yes, I do get offended, and I get tired of having to defend myself or of putting people in line. So now my attitude is: *I know what the hell I am, so I don't even need to waste my time and energy tripping off other people and what they think of me.*

I am very much a Californian by virtue of the fact that if you ask me, I will tell you my life story at the drop of a hat. Somehow I just have this natural ability to talk to people I don't know, in a friendly enough manner that usually makes them want to follow me home and see me to my door. This is not necessarily a good personality trait to have living in New York City. Paulette used to send me care packages of books to read on the subway and told me "not to leave the house without one," so as to not make eye contact with anyone. There's this stereotype of what a subway ride is like in New York: everybody sitting there reading something and not saying a word. If it were not for the loud-ass, one hundred-year-old train you could probably hear a pin drop. It's not a stereotype, I swear. I wanted to break out and say something out loud to break the silence several times, but, of course, I never did.

Speaking of trains, I missed the carpet and cushioned seats of B.A.R.T. *so* much during my stay in New York. The New York City subway system made B.A.R.T. seem like a Disneyland ride. I've been on the B.A.R.T.. train hella times when people were having conversations, and I've had conversations with people I didn't know on public transportation, not in New York though. I'm sure people would have thought I was a nut. Like they did the time I got sick on the train. To this day, I still can't figure out what the hell happened to me. I *do* know that on a crowded, rush hour train I had what felt like a hot flash, lost my vision momentarily and nearly fainted. Folks just looked at me like I was on dope or something. Nobody said a single word to me as I got off the train looking "shot to the curb," half my coat on and the other half dragging on the ground. I've had people say "bless you" when I sneeze on the train in Berkeley, so I was not used to this kind of treatment. But I chalked it up to "life in the big city." That and having to go through six or seven pay phones before finding one that worked and, more specifically, trying to find decent Mexican food. My friend Tonya and I were bugging so hard on an order of so-called nachos at so-called Mexican restaurants. People thought I was crazy, running around looking for burritos and tacos. (Juan's Place was one of the first stops I rushed to when my feet touched west coast soil.)

I gradually learned how to push my way onto an over-crowded train. I had to; it was either that or lose my job for being late everyday. The first time I took the rush-hour train to work I let three or four trains pass before I decided that I should probably get on one. I simply refused to push my way on to a train that had people packed in like sardines. That and having to barter fares with gypsy cab drivers were new experiences for me. After a couple of months I had become an old pro and rarely paid more than what I thought the fare should have been. Something about living in the city, particularly New York City, makes you a more forward and somewhat more aggressive person, not necessarily in a bad way, but I definitely noticed some changes. I'd catch myself rushing; I was constantly "rushing" somewhere. It was exhausting, mentally and physically. It would feel good to finally return to the regular "chill mode" of California.

Sometimes I think I just look like a nice person and that's what draws people to me. Only in New York, looking "nice" can mean looking like a sucker. I find that people in California tend to be much more warm and friendly than the folks I ran across in New York. Not every single person. I'm speaking in very general terms, of course. There are people who were nice to me right off in New York, and I've run into people in California I'd met at a party, and a week later, in public, they would purposely avoid making eye contact so they don't have to speak. Everyone I met in New York knew I was from someplace else from the minute we started talking. Most of them were guys who knew I was from somewhere else, they said, simply because I was talking to them. The women in New York have a reputation for being kind of hard. We have a much more relaxed attitude and response to things out west.

The pace is much slower in California, and the natural beauty of the place makes it easy to become a little spacey. When I lived in New York I realized how much of a "space case" I am. I constantly missed my subway stop from being in left field somewhere, day dreaming—a very dangerous frame of mind in New York. I call it being on automatic pilot or A.P. I got my wallet stolen in a bank once. I thank God for watching over me, because in New York (or any place else for that matter) a lot of things worse than that could have happened to me. That was the first of my two potential tragedies. The other was on the night I got into what I thought was a gypsy cab at 3 a.m. and realized that the driver was joy riding from Brooklyn to Manhattan and not a cab driver at all. I kept my cool though, and I'm proud of the fact that I didn't try to barter my fare with him. We wound up having an interesting conversation, and I think he even asked me for my phone number.

I'm not denying that there's a lot of crime in New York City. I'm just saying that I was fortunate enough not to have been involved with any of it, at least not anything serious. Lucky, I guess, since I'm sure I must have looked like "easy bait" half the time in what is supposed to be such a "crime ridden" place. After I moved back home to California, I experienced more crime in a year than I had in my whole life. If I had been on my P's and Q's in New York, maybe I would have felt that man going through my pocket for my wallet in line at the bank.

One of the highlights of my New York experience is the caliber of folks that I met there. When I moved back home I didn't feel the need to go back to New York to visit, because everybody I knew there came through the Bay Area—working. I'd met actors, musicians, dancers, actresses, etc., you name it, in New York City. Not folks just sitting around *talking* about what they were doing (or in my case what they "wanted" to do). They were "doing it." It was proof to me that the sky's the limit; nothing is unattainable if you are dedicated and put your mind to it. I met folks who were serious and accomplished in their chosen fields. I had never been encouraged to write and was made to believe that it was beyond my grasp to "make it" as a writer.

My friend Aziza is a dancer who supports herself financially doing just that. She had performed at the Metropolitan Opera House, had her own small company of young dancers, and had lived overseas teaching dance—she is a "dancer." Recently she opened a dance school for young kids called Precious Gems. Another friend, Lonnie, is a musician and has been self-supporting for the past twelve years, well known and respected in the New York music community. He has played with Art Blakey and the Jazz Messengers in the early eighties and is better known in Europe and Japan, where they appreciate real music. Demetria McCain is a sister who did her undergraduate work at NYU and by now has her master's in arts administration from Brooklyn College. She had started her own theatre company called Our Theatre: The Forgotten, and when I left New York, it was in her second season. Kevin Jackson is one of the most talented actors I've seen. He demonstrated for me what it means to have a real passion for your work. Garrett Fortner is the founder and publisher of a fly magazine called *New Word*. He started the magazine on his own a couple of years ago, and it has been pretty successful in the tri-state area. The list goes on and on. But the point I am making is that brothers and sisters had it "going on." It's a kind of "sink or swim" situation in New York. Not that I didn't know any people who were leading productive and creative lives here, it's just that in New York there is this "hustle" mentality that we just don't have, or let me say that I have yet to see in California.

Being an avid student of the arts, I could not have picked a better place than New York City for "cultural activities." There was so much going on all the time. The summer was the best because there were a lot of free things to take advantage of. I saw Art Blakey at JazzMobile and Denzel Washington as Richard III in the "Shakespeare in the Park" festival for free! My exposure to jazz tripled while living in New York. I frequented every place from Birdland to the Village Vanguard and the Village Gate, from Town Hall to small cafes and underground jam session spots. I'm not much of a night person, so I really didn't take full advantage of the club scene while I was there. Plus, I couldn't stand the fact that they pick and choose people to pay fifteen or twenty dollars to go in. New York clubs don't close at 2 a.m. In fact, people don't start going out until 11 or 12. By midnight, if I'm not already out, drink in hand, partying hard, I am not leaving the house. I grew to like house music, which I had hated initially and always thought sounded like '70s disco music. I suppose my appreciation for salsa and merengue can also be attributed to living in New York.

My personal interaction with African-American men was virtually nil before I moved to New York. For the first time in my life, I was dating. I felt like the belle-of-the-ball and very much like the beautiful African queen that I am supposed to be. The same way people talk about how beautiful the women are in California is the same way I feel about the men in New York. Brothers in New York are fine. It was quite a different sensation for me, because I got a lot of attention and had a lot to choose from. It was nice to be able to make eye contact and smile at black men and not be embarrassed when you discovered that he was smiling at the white girl in back of you.

I never felt the urge to do a high five when I saw a black couple; it was a very common thing in New York. I had people asking me if I was married. I'd never had this experience before and found it really interesting. As I would later find out, New Yorkers are a lot more family-oriented than people out west. I met people my age who were married or had been married before. In California, I didn't have any friends my age who were married. I bugged off of guys asking me whether I was married, thinking that it was their way of flirting until it happened more than once or twice. Then I realized that they were serious. In Cali, we just shack up.

> *I liked being in New York, but*
> *I think I really enjoyed just*
> *being out of California.*

People ask me if I want to live in New York again, and the answer is *hell, no*. I did that once. There are too many other places in the world to live. After having taken a bite of the "Big Apple," I feel like I could probably live comfortably in Guam if I had to. New York is a great place to visit, and I try to go back in September for the West Indian Day Parade on Eastern Parkway in Brooklyn every Labor Day. I often thought even if I were filthy rich, I would not want to live in New York City. I find that I have a preference for serene, tranquil, natural surroundings. Central Park is as close to that as I got in New York, and in the summer I spent quite a good amount of time there. I just made sure I was out of there before dark.

I always liked it here in California. After living in New York, life in California feels like a retreat. Growing up here is probably the reason that I'm a "fashion misfit." Dressing up in California means wearing socks or a new pair of jeans as opposed to faded ones. I've grown quite accustomed to being "casual." I also liked the fact that somehow I feel more motivated and obligated to lead a more healthy lifestyle when I'm here. It might have something to do with the weather, I don't know. California has it's problems and can be a bit superficial and shallow at times, but it's nice to look at, and at least it doesn't smell like a toilet in the summer. Oakland, in particular, has a lot of really wonderful qualities and, as I witnessed from my cross-country drive, there are a lot worse places to live, even in California, but I guess I'm a little biased since I was born and raised in the Bay Area. I never realized just how different other places in the country are until I went into a Quick Stop in Atlanta one Sunday and saw a mop handle stuck through the refrigerated doors where the liquor was kept. It went completely over my head at first. I could not even comprehend the idea of not being able to purchase alcohol on a Sunday. I had never heard of such a law before, so it was a totally foreign concept to me. At the time, I was buying orange juice (even in my wildest days, I didn't drink in the morning), but the thought of actually being forbidden to buy it tripped me out. I remember thinking: What if you're not a Christian?

When I heard that the budget for the New York State Department of Cultural Affairs, where I had been working, was being cut by forty percent, I knew it was probably time for me to go. I considered myself lucky since I had been able to work in the arts at least half the time I stayed in New York. I worked part-time doing administrative work at the Negro Ensemble

Company, the country's first Afro-American theater company, which was founded the year I was born, and later as a tutor to five child actors in the Broadway play *Mulebone*. They were both really wonderful experiences, and I met great people who helped me start actually enjoying life in the big city. After two years, I decided that unless you're doing something that you absolutely love or there is a specific reason you need to be in New York City, it's not exactly the kind of place you go to just hang out, just to be kickin' it. Life in New York was a struggle, the winter was horrid and seemed to last twice as long as the summer, but I still enjoyed being out of California. I wasn't really ready to go back home, but with no job prospects and no money, home to Oakland was my only option. Thanks to Paulette, the only person who knows that when I say I have no money it literally means *no* money, I didn't have to walk, she sent me a plane ticket to come home.

... to a friend

arrived at the San Francisco International Airport in early June dressed in a cotton mini skirt, tank top, and sandals. I guess I forgot where I was going. Summer in New York is nothing at all like summer in the Bay Area. I got sick the first week back home, in denial about the fact that summer in Oakland can mean wearing a sweater in the daytime. Oakland reminded me of *Boyz in the Hood*. After seeing blocks and blocks of what looked to me like an infinite number of brick buildings in New York, the streets of Oakland materialized like something out of a movie. Even more, Oakland reminded me of the south. I never noticed it before, but Oakland was country. I had a better understanding of what everybody had been saying and why they had been so insistent on my leaving. This city, where it's not uncommon to see a black person with blonde hair and finger waves, suddenly put me in mind of a west coast version of Tupelo, Mississippi. It didn't take me long to fall back into the don't-worry-be-happy-mode I had temporarily put on hold while living on the east coast. There was something different about Oakland that wasn't there before I left. I had always known there were unsafe areas of Oakland, sections where you couldn't walk without putting your life on the line, sections that I rarely went to. I came back home only to find that the whole city, including the neighborhood where I grew up, had become one of those "sections." Things had changed. I was afraid more often than I ever remembered being the entire time I lived there. What I was feeling prompted me to write a letter to my friend Tonya, who was living in D.C. We had graduated from high school together and have managed to keep in contact and maintain our friendship over the years.

June 2, 1991

Hey Girl,

What's up with you? So here I am, back in Cali. It feels good to be on familiar ground again, and now that I have a goal in mind and I'm shooting to do what I've been talking about for the past five years, I'm too excited. I had a ball living in New York. It's so totally different from out here, as you well know...I have to write about it one day. I'm happy to be back home, but hella shit has been happening that makes me think I should re-pack my stuff and move back to New York.

The past couple of months in particular have had me scared to death. I don't think I've ever been this afraid before in my life. You know how I'm always teasing *about my near-death experiences? I know you remember, my first one, when I choked on a margarita at Juan's and then that time I walked through that cow pasture near Stinson beach. Well, that was nothing compared to what I went through a couple of months ago. I was working part-time at Mailboxes Etc. on College Avenue in Berkeley and we were robbed at gun point. At ten o'clock in the morning, in broad daylight this man comes in, no mask or anything, with a gun, and demands the money. Motherfuckas are bold these days. I've <u>never</u> been that scared before in my life and he wasn't even pointing the gun at me. I was in a small closet-like room sorting mail when I heard Joy scream. The last thing in the world I expected to see was a man pointing a gun at her in front of the register. She must have looked over at me, because when I stepped back, he came over to the room where I was and told me to stay in there if I didn't want to get hurt. Girl, I could not even tell you remotely what he looked like, only that he was black and had a gun. He was a blur, it was like I lost my vision. After he left me he went back to the register and yelled at me to stay in there. If he only knew—I was frozen stiff with fear. There was a phone in the room with me and for about a tenth of a second I thought about calling the police. I also thought about trying to make a run for it. After that experience I can clearly see how people think and act irrationally in such situations. My face got numb, and I started thinking, I'm about to die. I just <u>knew</u> he was going to kill us. I figured that he was nervous about us seeing his face and was going to do away* with us to keep the police off his back. For those few seconds I <u>really</u> thought I was going die. It's true, I could have easily had my head blown off. I was freaking out and he wasn't even pointing the gun at me so I can't even begin to imagine what Joy must have been going through. (She told me she couldn't sleep for weeks after that—everytime she dozed off she saw that gun.) I was scared at first, then I got mad. Damn, a brother too. Why did he pick <u>us</u>? There are hella other businesses on College Avenue," which as you know is <u>the</u> white, yuppie neighborhood. It really fucked me up, because I was hella jumpy after that. I became really nervous if I had my back to someone for a long time, and I felt really upset that I had an involuntary, fearful reaction when a black man came into the store. It pissed me off that I could be scared of black men. I thank the Creator everyday because I sure did think it was my time to go that day. I've been extra scared because, like I said, Oakland has been fucking pandemonium these days.

The first two months of the new year, Oakland had a record breaking number of homicides, not in the Bay Area, just in Oakland. I was scared to watch the news because every time I did there was something horrible that happened a couple of blocks from my house or a place that I knew. You know that club on Shattuck called the Bos 'n Locker? Girl, somebody went in there and opened fire and killed a bunch of people. Then, too, hella car-jackings have been happening. But I guess the *incident that really fucked me up, well, the one for that particular month anyway, was a kidnapping that happened at the MacArthur B.A.R.T. station, yes, the same station four blocks away from my house, the same station that I used when I went back and forth to high school and college. A young black woman was forced into her trunk, driven to an ATM and then shot at gun point by a couple of teenage boys. Imagine that!!! All this happened during rush hour, four blocks from my house. Since I live so close to the station, I usually just walk home. It takes me between three and five minutes. Now I wait twenty to thirty minutes for a bus to go a couple of blocks. I hate it. It just so happens that I stayed at work late that day and decided to take the bus home. I could have actually been at the B.A.R.T. station when that shit happened, and I've been scared to death ever since. I think about the murdered woman everyday, twice a day, going to and from work. It could have been me. That shit bugged me out and kept me up a couple of nights. The young guys who did this turned themselves in a couple of weeks later. How's that for a psychological study? They kidnapped and killed a woman over a damn car and then couldn't take the pressure, so they turned themselves in. I don't think that was the work of serious gangsters. They're just a couple of disturbed young men who could obviously use some kind of psychological counseling, and in cases like this America's response to "mental help" is the penitentiary. Especially when it comes to black men. If the victim had been white, they'd probably be on death row right now.*

Speaking of the pen, I have had some really sad stuff happening in my own family. You know my brother is in prison, again. Well, my cousin Don is in too, in fact he's been in every since I've been back from New York. Anyway he and my brother were in San Quentin at the same time! Imagine that! I hate to be facetious but my immediate thought was "two ships passing in the night—my relatives and me." Oh, and at one point my biological father was in jail too. So I had three men in my family all in jail at the same time. To me, that shit was kind of deep. They are really pathetic. But one of them, I can't say which (I'm not trying to "dis" anybody), was out for only 24 hours, I kid you not! I thought about contacting the Guinness Book of World Records, *that shit has to be a record. Anyway, even though they are my family members, I am afraid of ex-cons. I understand what jails are designed for and how they can and do totally fuck people up. It's like, if you weren't crazy when you went in, you damn well might be when you come out. I knew my brother before he went to prison and did solitary confinement. I'm sure that he has changed, and, unfortunately, I don't think its for the better. It's a real serious issue with me these days. Every time he goes back I find myself being less and less sympathetic, even though I understand that he's becoming institutionalized and is probably more comfortable in there than out here. I feel really guilty and like some neo-Nazi conservative Republican sometimes for not wanting to be bothered with people in my family who look to me as if they are actually choosing to live a fucked-up, crazy lifestyle. And I get really annoyed and depressed being around people who are drunk all the damn time. It's a real negative vibe. I wish there was something I could do but they don't listen to me. They just think I'm a stuck up little goody-two-shoes. All I ever said was that I loved them and would love to talk and do stuff with them, but I refuse to do shit with a drunk. Get some help! They don't want help though. It's sad. I duck and hide sometimes when I see them on the streets.*

A couple of months after that kidnapping at the B.A.R.T. station, a good friend of mine was mugged and raped walking home from the Lake Merritt station. You know I was really bugging off that shit. She lived in the "good" part of Oakland and some motherfucker decided that he "wanted some pussy" and attacked her. I had heard about this kind of stuff happening, and, of course, I've seen it in the movies, but that was a quick reality check. I just couldn't believe this had happened to someone I actually knew. I don't consider myself a violent person, but I really thought we should find that asshole and shove a broomstick up his ass so he could understand what it feels like to be violated. Breaking a couple of bones or even killing the motherfucka could not make him atone for what he had done. I have a real problem with the system, and thought we should take matters into our own hands. As far as the "law" is concerned my friend is just another statistic, and the man who violated her is walking around scott free like he hasn't done any-

thing wrong. I was afraid, and every time I went in her neighborhood, I was looking at all the black men, wondering if one of them could possibly be the person who raped my friend. I had to catch myself. I'd be walking around with a serious attitude. It's a deadly combination, being angry and fearful at the same time. When my friend, who is usually an introverted, very private person, opened up and told me everything that had happened and what she was feeling, I was really relieved. I think it was very therapeutic for both of us, and I know for a fact that we are closer as a result.... Around that time several other women told me that they had been sexually assaulted. I guess I would never have known otherwise, its not exactly the kind of thing you discuss at the dinner table. So for a couple of months after that I was an emotional wreck, and all I could think was that if I was all fucked up, I couldn't even begin to imagine what my friend was going through. She knows what this man looks like. What would happen if she saw him again? I didn't get the sense that the "law" was looking for this guy.

I had a scary, disgusting thing happen to me one night too. It's hard not to be out at night when it gets dark at 5:00 or 5:30 p.m. I was standing at the bus stop, waiting to pay a dollar to go four blocks (which pisses me the fuck off), and this young black boy, he was over eighteen but definitely not deserving of being called a man, pulled out his dick and took a piss in front of me then tried to come over and talk to me: "What's yo name?" I felt like spittin' on him! Blatant disrespect. I couldn't believe it! I don't know whether this was worse than having that asshole in D.C. touch me on my butt—I had spent an hour in the hot, fucking sun, contemplating whether I should take my sweater off. I had on a new sleeveless body suit, and I was a little embarrassed because of my skinny ass arms, and as you well know, I don't usually wear stuff tucked in that brings attention to my ass. But it was ninety degrees and after an hour I thought to myself, "Fuck it, I'm taking this sweater off. Ain't nobody look ing at your bony ass noway." The minute I took the sweater off, this guy walked past me and touched my ass. You know I got pissed. I was just about to start calling him every black motherfucka in the book when an image popped in my head: I flashed to the night when I looked out my bedroom window and saw one of the neighbor- hood thugs beating the shit out of this woman. She was on the ground, and he was kicking her in the stomach, punching her in the face and dragging her in the middle of the street. I couldn't believe what I was seeing. It looked like a stunt scene in a Hollywood movie. Only her cries and screams for help made me realize that it wasn't a fucking movie. It was real life and right outside my bedroom window. My heart started racing, I got ner- vous and started shaking. I let go of the curtain in shock, probably hoping it would disappear, but I kept hearing her screams for help. My response was immediate: I flew down the stairs and out the front door. I don't know what I thought I was going to do, but just as I got out the door my grandmother nearly knocked out our front window telling me to come back in the house. I went back in the house right away to call the police, but I was out there long enough to see that our neighbors were on their porches watching the shit like it was a fucking show. I couldn't believe it. The girls next door to us were laughing. They thought the whole thing was funny. I didn't feel so bad for not having shit to say to them. My grandmother probably saved me from a real ass kicking.

A couple of weeks after I heard a man was shot to death two doors away from me, in broad daylight—the one Sunday I'm home. It's wild, I swear. There are block parties going on at one and two o'clock in the morning, on week nights! They don't care about the time and that people have to leave for work in the morning. I'm bugged that I have to be at work at 8:30 a.m. anyway and not being able to sleep because of car stereos blasting Too Short at all hours of the night pisses me the fuck off. As much as I hate the police, I've been tempted to call them more than a couple of times. So my neighborhood, and Oakland in general, are driving me crazy, for real. I'm tired of living in fear. But I ain't going nowhere, fuck it. I was born and raised in Oakland, and the last thing I want is to live around a bunch of white folks.

So, you can imagine that I've been counting my lucky stars, scratch that, I've been thanking God, everyday. That's a lot of shit to go through in one year. But it was a blessing not to have been victimized, not seriously anyway, in any of those circumstances. I might as well have been. It really trips me out though because Oakland, the blackest city in the Bay Area, has a bad reputation and the armed robbery and the mugging happened in "good" parts of the city. So it's been a hellish year. I can't believe I left New York and came to "laid-back" California to for all this shit. I've been scared to death. It's a trip because I'm down with my brothers, but Goddamn !!!

Love,
Aliona

menfolk

ultimate insult

The ultimate dis for a black woman, or one of the top five anyway, is to be dumped by a black man for a white woman. Not that white girls are all that. It's just that the idea of a black man being attracted to someone who prefers "them" is a slap in the face, an insult. If you're like me you think, only a fool would choose ground beef over filet mignon. Unfortunately, we have a lot of "fools" out here in California. We have them all over the state, and I'm convinced that they must originate out here and migrate to different parts of the country and the world. So, for more "insight," I made it a point to tune in to the *Oprah Winfrey Show* when the topic was "people who refuse to date inside their race." She had two black men on the show who refused to date black women, both of them were from California, need I say more...? But I really didn't need to watch Oprah to understand that. Hell, I know from personal experience.

Having been born and raised in California, I see a lot of interracial dating—it's as common to me as sliced bread. I didn't realize until I moved to the east coast that black men who prefer white women are not the "norm." A lot of black women see black men who prefer white women as an immediate rejection. Mediawise, white women are considered to be prettier and more feminine. A black man who has a preference for white women is reaffirming this ridiculous notion. As long as we place our self-worth in the hands of black men, and allow them to determine for us how attractive we are, we will always be upset. It's but another form of repudiation, of being unappreciated, only worse since it comes from our own men. It's behavior that reaffirms all of the negative stereotypes of black women. To have black men choose white women over black women can be extremely painful and a tremendous blow to the ego—as if we are not good enough. Especially for those of us who are convinced that we're "mo' better."

Sometimes it's not even about who's more attractive or easier to get along with. Some men, not just athletes and entertainers, see being with a white woman as a status symbol. In their minds, they feel like they have truly "succeeded" if they marry white, which, as far as I am concerned, is a goal for underachievers.

I was introduced to the world of "jungle fever" during my senior year of college. A good friend of mine, well, actually two good friends of mine, decided to fuck each other behind my back when I left town for spring break. Jennifer was a young white girl who had been a friend of my family. I knew she liked black men, but I didn't think she would mess around with somebody that I was interested in.

Greg Reeves was a brother that I met at a lily-white school in Pleasant Hill in our first semester of college. He grew up in a white suburb on the other side of the mountain, which should have given me an indication of where he was coming from. Despite my skepticism, I had a luke-warm friendship with Greg for three years. I never thought he would be attracted to me, because I didn't think I was his type, his "type" being ofays. By this time I was so used to the interracial dating idea that I didn't even take it personally. Later on he claimed he was attracted to me, but he didn't think I was interested in him.

Greg and I had a good relationship, and during my two-year stay at Diablo Valley College we became close friends. We studied together and critiqued each others papers. It was obvious he had very limited interaction with black people outside of his family.

I've always enjoyed men I can have a decent conversation with. In addition to being totally gorgeous, Greg was a great conversationalist. I enjoyed our platonic relationship. More often than not, most guys I met with were trying to get into my panties. I could appreciate him for not trying. Even though half the time I wasn't quite sure, because he had these inviting and alluring eyes. They were big and brown with lashes that were more straight than curled. He looked like he was inviting you to bed, but that was just his normal look. "Bedroom eyes," I guess.

He introduced me to the music of Jimi Hendrix and restored my confidence in my writing ability. He encouraged my writing, which I've always appreciated.

I considered Jennifer a good friend, and I tried very hard not to differentiate between her and my black girlfriends. I'd always heard that white girls had no regard for their female friends when a man was involved. But I thought that didn't apply to Jennifer because she was "different," and we were homies. We got along really well, and I didn't feel threatened by her being around men that I was interested in. Maybe I should have been. Have you ever heard the saying, "If you don't move you lose?" Well, girlfriend must have invented the phrase. Once, at a dinner party I gave, I caught her in a closet with her skirt up around her neck and a guy's hands between her legs. It just so happened that the guy, Brad, was someone that I was interested in. I thought he was interested in me too. I knew she was a little on the loose side, but didn't dream that she would screw Greg. I expected that kind of behavior from men, but not from *her,* my "friend." It never even crossed my mind that they were attracted to each other. And even if they were attracted to each other, she wouldn't sleep with him, because she and I were so close, and she knew that would hurt my feelings. Plus, I thought, Greg and I were just starting to explore the possibilities of getting involved, so I figured he was mine. Greg and I had developed this wonderful relationship, and for once, a man had taken the time to get to know me. I figured he liked me, and valued our friendship as much I had. So with those thoughts I felt confident about going away for spring break.

I was walking down the street near Dupont Circle in northwest Washington D.C. when I got this really strange feeling in my stomach. Then I got a feeling of disgust. I'd heard of " woman's intuition" but never really thought about it or allowed myself to fully experience it. I knew then that something was happening, or had happened, between Greg and Jennifer. I was suddenly consumed by anger. I managed to make it through the rest of my vacation without calling California. But as soon as I got back, I called Jennifer, and we had our usual small talk. Then I asked her if she had spoken to Greg, and she started crying. I started laughing because I *knew* it!!! And I knew what I was feeling was too strong to be wrong. She was crying and going on about how she really didn't want to, and how she has always had a problem saying no. I thought, "What a weak, simple bitch! What is *she* crying for?" I thought I should be.

I waited until I saw Greg at school to confront him about the whole thing. He took the manipulative/intellectual approach. He tried to convince me that *I* owed *him* an apology. Imagine that! His excuse was that we were not boyfriend and girlfriend. My friend? I thought. How sleazy. Since she was sleazy too (which is what I had decided after that Brad incident), I was starting to think they were a perfect match. Besides that, my attraction and respect for Greg diminished with every word that came out of his mouth. He went from being superfine to being just all right. I never realized how conceited he was until this incident. He was trying to imply that I was going to fight her over him. I am *not* the fighting type. I almost wish I was sometimes. Even if I were the fighting type, I would never fight over a man. Both of them should be happy that I'm not a violent person: The whole situation seemed grounds for kickin' somebody's ass.

Most black women have certain unspoken rules about stuff like that. Sometimes women are a trip when it comes to men. And as hard as it is for me to admit, a black woman, or any other kind of woman, is just as capable of behaving the way Jennifer did. We have some scandalous sisters out there too. I think the only difference is that we know what's "right" and "wrong," and in my opinion, some white girls don't, or maybe they do and don't care. If you are really "friends" you find out what the deal is *before* you go hopping into bed with somebody.

I was hurt for a couple of weeks even though, if I wanted, I could have gotten together with Greg. But that incident really showed me his true colors, and I became uninterested. He thought it would make me feel better if I knew that he didn't intend to have sex with Jennifer. All the time Greg and Jennifer were talking on the phone, Greg thought Jennifer was actually Jennifer's girlfriend (who was with her when they met Greg and me on a Berkeley corner in one day). Imagine that! When Jennifer showed up at Greg's door, he didn't even know who she was. He thought she was someone else: He had sex with her anyway. Well, she could have him. Besides, I was about to graduate from college. The last thing I needed was to be tripping over some fool who was into white girls.

I thought I would be devastated and totally depressed if such a thing ever happened to me. I figured my self-confidence would be shot. But not once did I feel like she was "better" than me or that I was less attractive than her.

That's the sad part about the whole thing: She didn't have to be anything but white.

Greg couldn't say that she was more interesting than me or smarter, since they were complete strangers to each other. The criteria for him was that she was white. A lot of times that's all that matters for some men. I just figured he was stupid—thanks to words of wisdom from my mentors. They had me convinced that men, young and old, black and white, and even the really smart ones, do dumb shit sometimes. Paulette told me that, unfortunately, it probably wasn't the last time I would have to deal with a man whose brain is in his trousers. The hardest part of it all was people telling me I was in denial, and that I was really hurting inside, that I was a "scorned woman." I was most hurt by the fact that I had developed this wonderful relationship with a black man, I thought, and he threw the whole thing over for this pathetic, scummy white girl. I really valued my friendship with Greg and considered our relationship special, since I had known him all through college. I felt betrayed though, like I could never trust either of them again. Trust is the basis of any relationship.

Since our families were friends, everybody we knew in common had heard about the incident and why we were no longer friends. I never quite understood why *I* was being made to look like some kind of shrew. Deep down I felt like somebody should warn Jennifer about the way she acts. She's going to try that act on the wrong black woman and get beat down. Some people do not play that shit. For some reason, this little, trampy white girl had everybody thinking that if we ended up at the same place at the same time I would beat her up. That was her own guilty conscious talking. I was not even thinking about her or Greg, especially since I had met and was having a good time with Derrick, who was a tenderoni visiting from Boston. It was really funny. No sooner had I finished telling the story to Derrick, when Greg and Jennifer came over. (I was rooming with her best friend.) It was quite fulfilling to introduce them to this gorgeous, intelligent brother who was as into me as much as I was into him.

I had a good friend in high school named Merritt Levine who was white and her boyfriend was black. Although she never actually said it, she had a "thing" for black men. Hell, maybe that's the reason she was friends with me in the first place: access to the brothers. "Once you have black, you never go back" was a phrase that pretty much summed up a lot of the white girls and their attraction to black guys. I really don't see anything wrong with them being together even though I, as a black woman, was single, wanting a boyfriend, and pretty much obsolete on the campus of Berkeley High School (and later Diablo Valley College and U. C. Berkeley). The general consensus is that white girls "gave it up" easier and put up with a lot more shit than any black woman would. Also, the standard of beauty in California is different; it's way too white. Brothers got these white girls thinking their shit don't stink, and if they try hard enough they can walk on water. Maybe its a "dick thang," and I just can't understand it. The brothers I knew were proud and boasted about their reputation in bed. They didn't see the sex stereotypes and myths about black people in a negative light the way I did. In fact, they laughed and said the stereotypes about black men weren't myths.

T he reason I never got together with a white guy was the same thing that made the black men popular, sometimes the most sought after in my high school. Aside from not wanting a white boy to use me to live out some sexual fantasy,

> *I've yet to meet a white male who didn't make me cringe when I thought of kissing him.*

Even during the times when I felt white men were paying much more attention to me than black men, I just couldn't get with that.

Three of my close friends have been seriously involved with white men. Of the three, only one has dated them on a regular basis. She doesn't have a preference for white men. Unlike the rest of us, she chooses *not* to date black men exclusively. Those of us who only date black men (and live west of the Mississippi) sometimes go for months on end being celibate, or dateless. With my friends, age is a contributing factor. When a black woman is upward of thirty-five, her hopes and dreams of meeting an honest, hard-working, supportive, affectionate black man who is willing to give, as well as receive, love and respect are almost nonexistent. Inevitably, a woman's standards drop and any man who is gainfully employed looks like Mr. Wonderful. Basically, men are men, and they all have problems. Obviously, black men have a whole different set of issues to deal with. But white men are far from being problem-free.

> *I love black men, but I am not planning to spend my whole life searching for love.*

On the other hand, I don't plan on settling for anything less than I deserve either. I can't imagine that my hopes and dreams of finding a black man will be completely dashed, but for some sisters, I'm sure they have been.

Sometimes I wonder if black men are affected the same way psychologically when they see us with a white man. It's a hard thing to swallow when you and all of your friends are single and "holding out" for the brothers, and they literally pass you by to get a white woman. I used to get a straight attitude and pissed when I saw a black man with a white woman. But now I'm like, "If he's with her, he probably ain't my type." And Lord knows, if I copped an attitude every time I saw a black man with a white woman, I would *stay* mad, because interracial dating is such a common thing in the Bay Area. I'm not into being angry or bitter, not all the time, anyway. Nine times out of ten, it seems as if black women don't choose white men for the same reasons that black men choose white women. I think a lot of black men choose and have a preference for white women because black men think white women are more feminine or are just plain superior to black women. But more often than not, when you see a sister with a white man, you can best believe she's been through the wringer with black men, or she's like me, and simply doesn't fit the mold. We don't have that certain look, style, or mind set that some black men like.

One of my friends came to California to work on a play, and she was seeing a guy in the cast, a tall, dark and handsome brother. She was sprung on him, and I guess he was on her too. Or maybe not though.... A couple of weeks after they arrived he dumped her for this white woman who had come to see the show. My friend told me about the night they met the woman. After the show, the white woman walked up to my friend and her man in the lobby of the theater and thanked them for a wonderful performance. My friend told me she was holding Mitchell's hand, so it was obvious they were a couple. My friend felt totally comfortable and confident, and not at all threatened that this white woman was complimenting and conversing with her man. I think black women are supposed to feel confident in such a situation. The thought of this white woman "stealing her man" never even crossed my friend's mind; the same way it never crossed my mind when I introduced Greg and Jennifer. At least I didn't have to listen to them screwing in the apartment right above me the way my friend did. Of course her ego was completely smashed. I told her about what happened to me, and I had also warned her about the brothers out here, although I didn't have to. All she had to do was take a look around, and she would find out what time it was. She's from D.C. and was not used to this shit at all. She could not understand what the white woman had that she didn't. In short, why he'd choose a white girl over her? My friend is smart and beautiful and has a great career ahead of her. Any man in his right mind would be honored to be with her. In short, she's a damn good catch, just as I believe myself and all of my friends to be.

It's not worth much if you're not the right color in America. I comforted her and told her that only in California would something like this happen.

I made her laugh when I said, "At least you get to go back east." Having had a similar experience, I could definitely relate. After living on the east coast and seeing how scarce interracial couples are, I could understand why she was bugging so hard. This was a totally foreign experience for her. She was not accustomed to feeling unappreciated by the brothers. In fact, all of my friends who visited me, wondered how I managed out here with all these brothers chasing white girls.

When I was in Kenya, I realized that the black man/white woman issue was a global one. Paulette, Melody, and I went to a bar, and upon entering, we went our separate ways. When we reunited we exchanged glances. We all had the same look of disgust on our faces. And then we laughed at the fact that without verbal communication we were all on the same wavelength. I was sure they had also seen the man at the bar dressed from head to toe in traditional Masai attire trying to rap to this white woman. He was in a serious gangsta lean position, with his elbow on the bar and his tongue practically in her ear whispering sweet nothings. She was probably the only white woman in the whole place, giggling and enjoying every bit of the attention she was getting. Paulette, Melody, and I looked at each other as if to say: *We came all the way to Africa to see this?* He probably travelled for days to get to the city, to see if he could get lucky with a European. And she was probably thinking about living out every wild, Mandingo sex fantasy she'd ever had.

I'm not a very spiritual person.

> *But I do believe that things*
> *happen for a reason.*

And I am a hopeless romantic, which is why I'm happy that Greg and Jennifer are still together today. I guess it was meant to be. I, more than anyone else can understand how difficult it is to find someone that you hit it off with. I learned that the moral of the story was "if it ain't broke, don't fix it." Greg and I had a perfectly good friendship. I learned that not every male-female relationship has to be a romantic one. I knew he wasn't my type, but ignored my intuition and decided to try and pursue him anyway. I know what kind of black man I want and as he demonstrated, Greg is not it. Some black men see being pursued by an ofay (for the wrong reasons) as an insult rather than a compliment. I believe in love, and I don't have a problem with people who genuinely fall in love with someone who just happens to be of a different race. But I'm talking about "jungle fever," having an interest in someone based on negative stereotypes or out of plain self-hatred.

The whole Greg-Jennifer experience was a learning one. I learned who my "real" friends were, and how strong I must have been to have endured such betrayal. Elaine, who is the quintessential optimist, told me that I should thank God for allowing Greg to show his true colors. As far as she was concerned, I was blessed that he hadn't been my boyfriend before I found out who he really was. I'm sure that if the incident had happened at an earlier point in my life, I would have responded the same way my east coast friend did when she got dumped for a white girl. Fortunately for me, I had already been shaped and molded by my three mentors, which is probably why I responded the way I did. Their prior nurturing and guidance made me feel like I deserved much more than he probably had to offer anyway. I wouldn't go so far as to say that I am glad it happened. However, I am glad that it shaped my sensibilities, a lesson I could share.

the brothers

There's something to be learned from everything we experience in life, even relationships. I think it's particularly important for men and women to be friends. I feel like there is so much we don't know and understand about each other. I've been fortunate enough to have had different kinds of relationships with men. From all of these relationships, I've learned a lot about myself and about life.

One of my most memorable experiences was one I still think about fondly. It happened almost ten years ago. I had been in Kenya less than a week when I met Saeed. Here was a man who thought I was a wonderfully beautiful person, and he didn't make me feel bad for not being ready to have sex right away. He couldn't believe that I wasn't seeing anyone and had never had a boyfriend before. He was seven years older than I was, and lived half way around the world and the whole experience was like something out of a movie.

I was in a club, and he just walked up to me from out of nowhere. Saeed made me feel special and made it clear that, although he was very attracted to me, he wanted nothing more than to show me a great time while I was in Africa. We spent practically every waking moment together, and we had a ball. We spent the days site seeing in Nairobi, meeting up with his friends for coffee at local outdoor cafes. At night, we went out dancing. Saeed was a perfect gentleman, and my "guardians" didn't mind me spending all this time with him. They sensed that I was in good hands. Paulette did anyway. Melody had her reservations about such a handsome, older man. He understood, and was used to, people being suspicious of him. Saeed was mixed, his mother was African and his father was Arab. He explained to me that a lot of people on the coast, in Mombasa, where he was from, looked the way he did. To my surprise, his being mixed was a hindrance. He was constantly harrassed by the staff at the hotel where I was staying. One night they actually refused to let him come to my room. We learned that they thought he was a terrorist, and that I had taught him Swahili, and he was planning to bomb the place. It was totally ridiculous, but the more we hung out the more I witnessed the kind of treatment he received. He assured me that things were different on the coast, and that I would like it much more than Nairobi. Despite the mishaps, the week we spent together was definitely one of the best times of my life. When he found out my trip to Italy had been cancelled, he assured me that this was God's way of saying we were supposed to spend that week together.

When it came time for me to leave, I was miserable. I thought we would never see each other again. It took going half way around the world to find a man who showed me what it's like to be loved. There was no doubt in his mind that we would see each other again. I could appreciate his optimism. But since he had never been out of Africa, and the next time I visited I'd have to pay for it myself, I was a little skeptical. We spent the next three years writing each other diligently. Five years later, we were reunited. By this time I was living in New York and practically bald. Actually we hooked up in Canada. He seemed not at all phased by my new look, and he told me that I was just as beautiful as when we first met at the nightclub in Nairobi. We picked up where we left off, only this time it was different because I wasn't a virgin, which gave me permission to rock his world. I spent my birthday with ten gorgeous African men who bought me a cake and some ice cream and sang happy birthday to me in Swahili. The whole experience was the first time I understood what Paulette meant when she said "never say never." I never thought I would make love to a married man, in fact I used to swear that I would never do it. As Roz puts it, "I'm not trying to get bad marriage karma."

If I'm such a hopeless romantic, and I totally believe in love, and I'm in love with the idea of being in love, then why is it that I spend more time alone than in a relationship? I spend more time alone than anyone else I know, which is kind of ironic since I consider myself so "fly." And even more interesting question is why it is that of the three monogamous relationships that I've had (yes-three, count them, one-two-three) they've all lasted roughly eight months, give or take a few days. Eight months! I have never had a monogamous relationship that has lasted longer than eight months. This number eight applies to boyfriends only, flings and in-betweens not included. I need to go to a numerologist and try to find out what the number eight has to do with my love life and why it keeps coming up. With my luck, it probably means that I'll be single until I'm eighty or I'll get married eight times or that I'll have eight kids.

There are several answers to my questions about being single most of the time. The most obvious would be my preference for black men. Actually, it's not even that I "prefer" brothers. I just refuse to go out with anybody else. Only lately have I begun to wonder if I'm hanging myself or setting myself up for something I might be sorry for ten years down the road. I've yet to meet a man of another race that I can see myself getting intimately involved with, even though my experience with African-American men was practically non-existent before I moved to the east coast.

> *Sometimes I wonder if I'd be crazy enough to pass up a man who could make me happy because he was not black.*

For some reason, I just did not attract black men who were worth my time. More often than not, the ones with whom I had things in common and could hold decent conversations were into white girls. So all through high school, and my first year of college, I didn't date or have a boyfriend. In the ninth grade one of my classmates signed my year book: "To Aliona, you are a very nice young lady, now we just need to find you a boyfriend." I was really embarassed, I could not believe she wrote that. It made me wonder just how many other people noticed my situation. I felt like it wasn't my fault. The "brothers" just didn't like me. I was either too black or not black enough.

It was probably around that time in my life when I first started to wonder whether I was attractive. With age comes wisdom, which, combined with my developing cynicism, gave me a new attitude: I decided that it's not me, it's them. Just because my look doesn't appeal to them doesn't make me ugly. Somehow I just didn't see an "ugly" person when I looked in the mirror. It wasn't until my second year in college that I had a boyfriend, before him I had very little interaction with men. My biggest concerns, when it came to men, were not being sincerely appreciated or being dogged by somebody, so I just simply did without. But I ended up getting dogged anyway.

I've only been involved with men of African descent. I took ethnics studies class at Cal, and I remember we discussed interracial relationships. When I didn't raise my hand in response to being involved with someone of a different race a classmate replied, in total shock, I might add, "For real girl, I just *knew* you had." I was actually offended and thought: "Damn, what did I ever do or say that would make her think I would be involved with an ofay." Some of my friends used to tease me about only liking Africans. Most of my interaction with men was with Africans from the continent. I didn't exactly choose *them*. I like black men, but I couldn't help the fact that Africans found me more appealing than African-American men. My feeling was that anybody who could hold their own in a conversation with me, and keep my attention, had a shot with me. In junior high and high school, the fact that I was flat-chested and not "putting out" was not exactly in my favor either. If I had made myself available to white boys, I probably could have dated and even went to the senior prom, but it was just not that kind of party with me.

I've always been super-selective when looking for a "mate." I like men who are smart, which makes me think of Wandele, whom I met when I was in my preppie mode. He was very studious, quite articulate, and a damn good actor. He even went to church. He told me he was in exile from South Africa. I got the impression that if he had been born in this country, he probably would have been a Republican. He had majored in business and would act extremely conservative at times. Unlike a lot of the other South African students, around at the time, he didn't drink or smoke, and he re-assured me that he wasn't into ofays. He was straight and seemed to be absolutely wild about me. We had a good relationship. But initially I wasn't attracted to him the way he was to me. When I suggested that we just be friends, he started crying, and in doing so, he made me cry. So I agreed to give him a chance. I think I was impressed by his ability to cry in front of me. Here was a man who wasn't embarassed to show such emotion in front of a woman, which was a definite plus with me. He grew on me and three months into the relationship, at 19, I had sex for the first time.

So here I was in this great relationship with a great guy. My parents, family and friends all loved him. We studied together and planned to transfer to Berkeley at the same time. Everything was fine. It was our eight-month anniversary, however. I was enjoying my ballet class, when I noticed a woman walking by, peeking in, trying to look discreet but not doing a very good job. I noticed she was checking me out, so after she peeked inside for the fifth or sixth time, I decided to find out what her problem was. I stepped out the door and asked in my soft, semi-shy voice, "Do I know you?" That one question opened the flood gates of an experience that would be forever known as the Bermuda triangle. Alicia, that was her name, and I started talking and comparing notes, and I found out that she had been sleeping with Wandele the entire time he and I had been dating. Apparently they were involved before I came into the picture, and she thought that by sleeping with him she could get him back.

My feelings were hurt, and I was angry. I was appalled by the idea that this guy was dogging me. Alicia and I decided to double-team his ass and make him pay for trying to be a womanizer. Not once did I stop to think: What does *she* have to gain from helping me to get back at him? At this point, I didn't care about any of that. I was devastated. Being the young, näive woman that I was, I tried to be civil and to approach him about what she'd told me. Wandele categorically denied everything. He told me that she was jealous of our relationship and was just trying to break us up. I told her what he said, and she said that he was lying. In fact, she claimed to have been telling me all this out of "sisterly love." I didn't know which one of them to believe and spent several sleepless nights trying to figure out which one was lying. Just when I was about to trust my boyfriend and ignore this strange woman who walked up to me off the street, damn near, the shit hit the fan!

A Nigerian friend of his told me that he walked into Wandele's house and caught him in the bed with Nandi, a young South African woman who had just moved to the states and was staying with him until she got on her feet. Of course, he denied that too. I was too through. According to him, people were telling me this stuff to break us up. He claimed that the Nigerian guy wanted to get in my drawers. I decided to hook up with Alicia and get back at him: I'll teach his ass, he will think twice the next time he tries to fuck with a sistah from Oak-town. The whole incident brought out a side of me that I didn't even know existed. Quite simply, I wanted revenge.

Alicia and I made a plan. She was totally cooperative. I called him, apologized for being so silly and told him that I wanted to see him after our night class because I had a surprise for him in the library. So, later we trotted over there arm in arm. We got off the elevator on the third floor and walked over to a table where the "other woman," Alicia, was sitting with her comrade. The comrade was Shiree, who was about five feet tall and weighed a hundred and ten pounds. She was back up ammo in case he wanted to get stupid and we had to *STOMP* his ass. I walked him over to the table and announced to the entire floor of the library that he was busted and that he had better start explaining or I was going to get real hoogie. When I saw that everybody stopped studying, I put on my drama hat and clowned his ass right there in the Laney College library. I knew that public humiliation and embarrassment were his pet peeves. I asked him if he knew Alicia and told him she had given me all of the other juicy details about their affair. "Somebody is lying," I said, "and we're getting to the bottom of this mess right now." He stood there looking as though fire might come out of his mouth. He didn't say a single word; neither did she. I was doing all the talking and having a ball. For probably the first time in his life, Wandele had nothing to say. I was all in his face, laughing and enjoying being the center of attention. It was an out-of-body experience: I turned into a maniac and temporarily lost my mind. I could not believe that he was trying to play me for a fool and more importantly had been lying to me. I was insulted that he thought I was dumb, and that he thought he could actually get away with this shit. After about five minutes (it was probably only two minutes), he finally turned around and walked away with his tail between his legs—probably one of the wisest decisions of his life. If he was embarassed by my getting loud, he would have really been embarrassed getting his ass kicked by three women.

Alicia, Shiree, and I had a good laugh, then went to have a cappuccino to congratulate ourselves on a job well done. To me, getting even, the way I did, was the best revenge. For a couple of weeks after the whole thing, I thought I would burst into tears. (That's what people do when they break up, right?) While I was waiting, I was also watching my back. Days, weeks, and finally a few months passed, and I didn't shed a single tear. I didn't have time to be stressing over him or anybody else. I graduated from junior college and was on my way to Berkeley.

A couple of years later, I went to Wandele's graduation party in Los Angeles (I had clowned him so bad that he transferred to U.C.L.A. instead of Berkeley). And of course he asked me out, but I laughed in his face. He ended up going back to South Africa (I heard he was working for the government there). Alicia and I became the best of friends. Our friendship is one of the few positive things about that whole episode. Even to this day, we laugh when people ask us how we know each other. I introduced Alicia to my mentor Paulette, who said she got weird vibes from Alicia. Paulette says that people have to earn your trust, and she still thinks I'm crazy for believing Alicia. But in this case I trust my own judgement. What a way to get introduced into relationships though. What a way to get introduced into relationships. I suppose I wasn't in love with Wandele. Had I been, I would have taken the whole thing a lot harder. I'm resilient. A month after, I was back to my old self.

It wasn't until I went to New York and met B.J. that I had another boyfriend. (It probably would have been Greg Reeves, but he dumped me for that white girl, Jennifer.) I always say you can learn a lot about a person by the type of music they listen to. When I first met B.J. he had two suitcases of compact discs and not a single one was by a black group. I found that a bit strange but decided to give him the benefit of the doubt. He seemed like a nice guy and was a perfect gentleman. I'm always a sucker for those types. He was an excellent cook and often made dinner for me. He would set the table with silverware, linen napkins and all: I could get used to this. I'll never forget our first date. It was the most fun I'd had in a long time. I read in the *Village Voice* that Milt Hinton was playing at a piano bar in the West Village. I decided it was a perfect opportunity to ask B.J. out and expose him to some real music. He had never been to hear live jazz before and was excited about coming. This was a definite plus with me, since I remember getting into an argument with Wandele just about going to a museum. He had never been to one before and refused to go on those grounds. So, I went to the Jacob Lawrence retrospective at the Oakland Museum by myself.

B.J. and I met at Zinno's, and he had a dozen beautiful irises for me when I got there. After the first set, Milt Hinton came over to us (the only other black people in the joint) and started talking as if we were old friends. In my usual, sly, observant manner, I checked B.J. out. I really liked how comfortable and confident he appeared to be in a room full of white people. At the time, I didn't know that it could also be a problem. Later I found out that he was more comfortable in a room full of white people than he was with black folks. But, I liked him and decided to make it my job to "enlighten" him. After all, I thought, "what could you expect from a black person raised in England?" My roomates called him weird and swore that his accent was fake. They said that he exaggerated the way he pronounced certain things. They couldn't believe that I thought that was the way he really spoke. We had an interesting relationship, and I was spoiled rotten. He worked a lot, so when we did spend time together it was usually in the evenings. He was at work all day on the weekends, so for nearly eight months(!) my Saturdays and Sundays were spent in his studio apartment in Brooklyn listening to the new jazz CD's we bought. It was winter and usually too cold for me to even *think* about going outside, so I stayed in. He had only ever heard of Bird, Monk, Trane and Duke, so I bought all that stuff. While I was trying to educate his ears to the sound of America's pre-eminate art form, I was also learning new things. My knowledge and appreciation of jazz flourished. I could not have picked a better place than New York City for this type of exposure. It was during this time that I developed an interest in learning to play the upright bass, having met my friend Lonnie, a popular and very talented bass player in the city. We spent hours on the phone developing what would turn out to be one of my most fufilling relationships. We had a big brother-little sister relationship. I lived vicariously through him, and I picked his brain for every detail of his world travels and experiences playing with some of the jazz greats.

B.J. was a good guy, and God knows he was hella good to me. He showered me with presents and surprises, which did not make me like him more, or less, because I pride myself on not being a materialistic person. Every Sunday evening he came home with a wonderfully wrapped trinket from the fancy, over-priced Soho store he managed. In addition to cooking for me and washing my clothes, on his only day off, he was also very nurturing emotionally. He stayed up with me when I had nightmares and let me talk them out with him. Basically, it was a good relationship. What happened, you ask? Why aren't we together today? Why didn't we get married and live happily ever after?

Generally speaking, I'm a pretty tolerant person, and it takes a lot to make me angry, but I do have a couple of things that will incite instant rage. He had already pushed one of my buttons, but since I have a tendency to over-react, we discussed the situation, and I forgave him. But this time I had to drop him. He lied to me about using cocaine. I knew he had previously indulged, and I didn't have a problem with that, especially since he told me he was completely over that phase of his life. However, we had a birthday dinner party for my roommate at a restaurant, and B.J. goes in the bathroom with another man and is in there for twenty minutes. Okay, maybe it wasn't exactly twenty minutes. But I was on my period, had cramps, and really didn't want to be out in the first place so it felt like twenty minutes to me. I went over to the bathroom door to wait for him to come out so we could talk in private. I wanted to know what took him so long. He came out and didn't even see me standing there as he walked right past me. When I asked him if he had used cocaine in the bathroom, he told me no—with a straight face—acting totally insulted. But I'm no fool. I knew he had, and he pushed one of my buttons: he lied. I can deal with a lot of shit from a man but dishonesty is not one of them. If he had told me the truth, we'd probably be together right now. Well, maybe not, but at least we'd be friends. It would have been a nice break up. There is such a thing, right? So we did go our seperate ways, and six months later he confessed to having used cocoaine that night. He lied, because he was afraid that I would get angry. I got angry anyway, so what was the point of lying?

The real drama with B.J. didn't start until after I moved back to California. Thank God I did, or else I might not be around to tell this story. He seemed like such a harmless type of guy. That was one of the things I liked the most about him. He was a physically large but quite gentle. He was so large that sometimes people actually moved out of his way when we walked down the street. I guess he represented peoples' biggest fears: a hulking, dark-skinned, black man. If they only knew. They had no idea that he was probably the most harmless person thcy'd ever meet. Nobody would have believed me if I told them that he was afraid of cats. But he was scared of cats the same way I am of snakes. I didn't think it was nearly as strange as I do now. But he was about 6 ft. 4 in. and well over two hundred pounds, on the verge of being fat. His waist line looked like he had swallowed an intertube.

When I was unemployed and financially strapped, back in Oakland again, I get this phone call from him *insisting* that I send him three hundred dollars and the black suede overnight bag he had bought me. He was being sued by American Express, and he demanded that I send him money to help pay the court costs. But he decided to be *nice* about the whole thing and not charge me interest, and he would even accept partial payments. I was convinced that he had completely lost his mind. I had no idea what the *hell* he was talking about. I never once asked him for anything, and I knew for a fact that I didn't take any money from him. I figured this was his masculine way of asking for help, but his pride and ego would not let him simply ask to borrow the money. He started harassing me and calling me at work, and, at one point, spoke of coming to California to get his money if he had to. He called me and threatened to break my neck. I got really scared until I realized that I have a bunch of really crazy people for relatives, just waiting for an excuse to act the fool. I thought to myself, If he thinks he has problems *now,* let him come out here trying to fuck with me. He really will have some problems. He had hit rock bottom. He had lost his job and his apartment. And was calling me, going on about how everybody he'd met in his life had used him, including me. Although I felt sorry for him, I really flipped out, thinking that he was crazy, and that I used to be intimately involved with this man.

That thought scared me. It's like, how do you know when people are crazy? You don't. B.J. could have gone fifty-one-fifty on me. I couldn't believe it. He seemed so normal when we were dating. For a while I was scared to answer the phone, thinking it was him. I was actually relieved when it was a bill collector. Everybody has to have at least one lunatic experience in their life. I heard B.J. was deported back to Trinidad.

I really have to be careful about what I say to people, especially men. They can't take honesty all the time. I can be too honest sometimes. I never say things to intentionally hurt people. And to this day, I cannot understand why James took offense to my telling him that I was bored with him sexually. If I cared about a man and he was bored with me sexually, I would work to improve our physical relationship. I don't even think I was "bored." I was just not as attracted to him as he was to me. I liked James, and grew to care for him a lot, but I was not nearly as serious as he was. He was family-oriented, and he really wanted to settle down and get married. At that particular time in my life, I was not thinking about marriage. I should have made him aware of this from the start. I guess he felt like I was leading him on; naturally, I didn't see it that way at all. I enjoyed his company and liked the idea that he adored me, and that he would do anything for me. I guess I got kind of comfortable. James was a very trusting man. I never felt like he was lying to me or telling me one thing and doing another. I wanted to get married, but I guess my common sense kept me from jumping at this particular chance to get hitched. I know there are some people who would have loved having that kind of security, especially if they had the kind of track record with men that I have. But I didn't feel like it would be my last chance to get married. If I'm still single even ten or fifteen years from now, I'd like to believe that I wouldn't jump at a chance to get married if he's not "the one."

I hate breaking up on bad terms. My feeling is that this person is someone I've spent time with and have been intimate with. The least we can do is try to maintain a friendship. As I found out with James, some men are incapable. They don't know how to be friends with women. That hurt my feelings more than the fact that we broke up.

I consider myself such a good person that I don't quite understand why anybody would *not* want to at least be friends with me. He didn't want to. James was my first African-American boyfriend. I liked him, because he accepted me for the reasons I think most African-American men *don't* like me: I'm a natural-looking kind of a woman. James didn't mind that I didn't try to look like an *Ebony* fashion fair model all the time. I think he appreciated the fact that I had my own sense of style and my own standards for myself. He understood perfectly how it was for me not feeling appreciated by black men, because even though we never talked about it, he had the same problem with black women. He had a great body, and after we broke up, I regretted that I never told him that. He was a really nice guy, but somehow that wasn't enough. But I decided I can't be with a man just for the sake of having someone in my life.

Call me crazy, idealistic or whatever, but I would like to be appreciated for being the wonderful person that I am, not for my body. This attitude will probably keep me single well into my fifties! I've been told over and over by my older friends that they have found that no matter how much they have accomplished, or how smart they are, men still choose and judge women on the basis of how women look. How women "look" and how we feel about the way we look should be determined by us and no one else.

So as I write this, I am, as I have been most of my adult life, single. Surprisingly enough, being a hopeless romantic and all, I've grown used to it. In my old age, I've learned never to "settle." I know that one day (probably when I least expect it) I'll meet a man who will see beyond all of the superficial stuff and fall in love with the "real" me. All I ask from a black man is that he be honest, affectionate, supportive, intelligent, hard-working and willing to give as well as receive love and respect.

family, mentors
and me

family portrait

When Roz was telling me about her family, I remember thinking: Damn, don't they have *any* fuck-ups? Her brother had just graduated from Meharry Medical School and was about to do his residency at Harlem Hospital; her older sister is an attorney; her youngest sister, a classically trained ballerina, was about to enter her freshman year at Howard University; and Roz, the most academically "unstable" of the bunch, had just graduated from the Yale Drama School, having done her undergraduate work at Howard (graduating with honors, of course) and already appearing on Broadway. Her dad is a professor at a nationally known university, and her mother is no less than perfect, I'm sure.

I didn't even know her family, but I felt so proud of them. I kept saying to myself, these are black people, African Americans. I thought about all the people who complained that *The Cosby*

Show was totally unrealistic, because they couldn't conceive the idea of a black family with a doctor *and* a lawyer, two professional people, as heads of the household. I guess folks are so used to seeing families like the one in *Good Times* that a halfway positive image becomes unreal. To be a black family doesn't mean you have to be broke and down 'n out, a car jacker or welfare recipient.

Black America does have a middle class. Many black families in this country have second- and third-generation college graduates, own businesses and property passed down from generation to generation, and are pretty affluent citizens of our communities. I knew educated, professional black people before I met Roz; only the folks I knew were mostly single, black women trying to figure out where their male counterparts were hanging out. I know what you're thinking, and get that thought out of your head! These women were not necessarily looking for Mr. Corporate America, but he did have to be at least gainfully employed.

Not so long ago it was against the law in the United States to teach a black person to read. This was a tactic used (quite effectively, I might add) to keep black people oppressed.

I was amazed to learn that as early as the turn of the century, black colleges began to flourish, producing black doctors, lawyers, engineers, inventors, scientists, scholars, and educators who would go on to make invaluable contributions to this country. But some folks were too busy trying to "make it" from day to day for school. I remember asking my friend Joy why had she waited until she was thirty-four to get braces, why she hadn't gotten them as a child? Her response was, "I was too busy trying to eat." I thought about that comment in relation to my own family.

I come from a working-class background, where, with the deaths of both my grandfathers, the work ethic simply vanished (for the men anyway; the women always have managed to hold their own).

My grandfather on my mother's side is my earliest recollection of a male influence. His name was Stephen Robinson, and in his heyday he looked like Ricky Ricardo (Desi Arnaz). He was born and raised in Shreveport, Louisiana. A quiet, almost shy man, he'd cook, clean, and baby-sit at home while still working hard to make sure his family was well provided for. For twenty-five years he worked for the naval air station and never missed a single day. When I look at the other men in my family now, I find it hard to believe they are cut from the same cloth. I have never been attracted to men who feel the need to wear their "manhood" on their sleeves: gangsta, thug, and slickster types. Although I hadn't thought about it much, memories of my grandfather are probably the reason certain types of men appeal to me—kind, gentle, hard-working men.

My grandmothers are women of tremendous strength and endurance. I'm amazed that neither one of them has been committed or locked up for taking somebody out. My maternal grandmother "wore the pants" in her family. Fortunately, she married a man who was above dishing out b.s. Even if he did,

my grandmother is the kind of woman who wouldn't have stood for it, not for a minute. A man wouldn't even try to get stupid with her. Raising a hand to hit *her* would have been a death wish. My grandmother is very independent, with an incredible sense of self-worth. She was happily married and loved her husband very much, but would have made it with or without him. She was the disciplinarian and, from what I understand, would give you a whipping while she was lying in the bed, daring you to move. But I guess she ran out of gas by the time she got to the grandchildren, because I never saw that side of her—except for the time when I was about six or seven, and she caught me and my cousin D.C. smoking in the backyard. Maybe I never saw that side of her because I rarely did anything that deserved getting beat. She told me that my mother and I were the same way as children: scarey and timid. The sound of the child crying in that Temptations song "Runaway Child" was enough to frighten me to death. That and a fire engine or ambulance siren. I remember leaving my tricycle at the corner of 39th and Market when a fire truck went by. I actually left the bike there and ran home crying. I was also known for pulling out a fist full of my own hair when I got mad as a toddler—perhaps the genesis of my career in hair demolition.

The folks in my family think I'm strange. On several occasions family members have told me that I "act white," and one of my aunts asked me, suspiciously, if I wanted children. I know I have a tendency to be a little sensitive, and I over-react sometimes, but I really took offense to her asking me that. I thought to myself, why the hell *wouldn't* I want kids? I couldn't understand why she would ask me such a question. After giving it some thought, I still had an attitude, but at least I understood some of the motives for the question.

I'm the only woman in the whole family over eighteen who doesn't have any kids! It's really a trip, because even all the little girls I used to baby-sit when I was a teenager are now mothers—all except one. Fortunately for me, I have my own agenda. I'm in no rush to join the ranks of motherhood. I feel like I'm too young to be a mother. I'm just not ready for that yet. Besides, I would like to be married first. I don't plan on raising children by myself. I know that sounds like a fairytale to some folks, but I don't think its a far-fetched notion. It seems ridiculous to people in my family, because everybody's been doing it the other way for so long it's become the norm. When my mother was my age she already had two children. My closest cousin is only two years older than me, and she is deep into motherhood and family. I don't feel old or pressured, but I guess compared to everyone else in the family, and judging from the way it's been done in the past, I am a little bit "over the hill." I took offense to my aunt's question because she just assumed that I didn't want children. It just makes me feel like they think something is wrong with me when I get asked weird-ass questions like that. Maybe she thinks I'm gay or something. I guess I shouldn't be surprised, since "conveniently" I never seem to be dating anyone around the time we have family gatherings.

In his little sorry-ass attempt to make me feel like I had some problems, my stepfather accused me of having "lesbian tendencies." The fact of the matter was that he had *no* idea what I was doing or with whom. I've always been a relatively private person, and what I do is none of *his* damn business. According to him, because I seemingly wasn't having sex and sleeping around, I was a lesbian. If I *had* been sexually active (responsibly or not), he would have called me a whore.

> *With some people you can't win for losing, so it's better to just go by your own program and pay folks no mind.*

I'm too young to be somebody's mother. More importantly, I'm not *ready* to be somebody's mother—yet. All I ask is that folks respect that. I'm tired of the issue of my having kids *now*. But they're really going to be too through if ten years from now I still don't have any kids or, God forbid, decide I don't want any at all or that I want to adopt. I don't want to be a single parent, but as I have seen with my own eyes, sometimes the situation is unavoidable. For being a relatively private person I've been labeled "goodie-two-shoes." They don't know the half of what I do, and I like it like that. So I don't mind the label. It's funny to me.

When I was in my junior or senior year of college, probably around the time I was thinking about dropping out, I ran into another aunt, and when she asked what I was doing with my life, I said that I was still in school and she responded "Well, if that's what you *like*...." Excuse me??? Whoever said anything about like. I have always enjoyed learning, but I have never *liked* school. Even though college was a choice for me, I wasn't there because I it. I did it because at eighteen I wasn't doing anything else with my life, and I was *not* into getting a job that I would stay with forever. By the time I transferred to Cal, it became a personal goal, going to college. I realized that we didn't have any college graduates in our family, so I decided to become the first. I couldn't believe that my aunt thought I was in school because I *liked* it. Hell, most people don't work because they *like* it, it's just something that you have to do. That remark kind of confirmed for me how I thought some folks saw me— as a nerd! Because my business is not in the street, they don't think I do a lot of stuff.

My friend Joy told me she had the exact same reputation in her family. For being the first person to go to college in her family, for having goals and aspirations, she was accused of "thinking she was better" than everybody else. She made it known that she wanted a better life than the one she grew up with. That was a mistake! It didn't help that she wasn't "fast" and was more into school than boys. She was "square." In my family, because I don't drink (during the middle of the week), I'm a square. If they only knew. I have been fucked up more times than I care to remember. Fortunately, it was only a phase, and I got bored with it quickly. But hanging out with white kids, getting drunk was an actual social event. Now I'm pretty much a social drinker, so occasionally I'll have a few gin martinis or a shot of Cuervo Gold. I'd probably go into a coma if I tried to keep pace with what I used to when I was in high school. Old English smells like pee, I cannot believe I used to drink that stuff.

There's a person in my family whose goal in life is to make other people miserable. Until recently I used to be able to deal with her, but about a year and a half ago we had a falling out, and I haven't spoken to her since. I try to keep my life free of negative people, male or female, family or friends, since there are so many elements in society that we don't have any control over. So when it comes to something I *can* control, I do everything in my power to deal with it appropriately (maybe this is a new younger generation attitude). Anyway, this particular relative is mean and nasty, and if you let her, she will tear you down. She made me cry, telling me that I "thought I was white," or I "acted white." I don't remember which, but something to that effect. I *do* remember that it took me two days to stop crying. That hurt my feelings like nothing I'd experienced before, especially coming from someone who had known me all of my life (it did "wonders" for my self-esteem). And it happened around the time I was really disgusted by white folks, so I was *really* insulted by the remark. She was basically calling me an "oreo," the kind of black person who sees being born black as a curse and, if given the chance, would be white. It wasn't until I took the time and energy to really think about it that I understood what was going on.

Fortunately, I live in my head a lot. I am always tossing and turning ideas around and trying to analyze and figure things out. So this time, when I finished crying, I thought about it and decided that I was not like a white person, in any way, shape, or form. Black people have been brainwashed so badly that we have this totally negative and stereotypical idea of what it means to be black, and if you are not seen in that image, then you're trying to be something else. It's a pathetic way of looking at things, but it's true. Because I have goals and aspirations, trying to do something with my life, I'm "trying to be white." My relative wouldn't have been able to condemn me if I was like everyone else in the hood. If I wasn't trying to better myself, not living my life to the fullest, then I would be "acting like the black person I am." Some people who talk that nonsense are the same ones who run to get their hair relaxed like clockwork, every six weeks, because they can't stand new growth or a nappy kitchen. Her comment really made me wonder how other people in my family viewed me. All I want is to be a positive role model to my younger cousins, and so far, I feel confident enough to say that I'm doing just that. I wouldn't argue that they probably think I'm different, maybe even weird, but I know for a fact they don't think I'm like a white person. If anything they probably think I'm like a Rastafarian, or that I'm stuck in a time warp.

I hate being called "bourgie." In my opinion, it has a negative connotation. To black folks being *bourgeois* means having an interest in things that are uncommon and stuff that "regular" black folks don't partake in. *That's* not bourgeois to me. One friend put it best. He said that a bourgie person is one who lacks consciousness. I agree with that definition, and it makes me proud to say that it doesn't include me. Being bourgie means putting on airs and thinking you're better than other people or judging people by how much money they have or what kind of car they drive. Just because I like stuff that they don't, the relatives say that I "act white," and therefore bourgie. I'm the most down-to-earth person anybody could ever meet. A lot of the things I like to do are very middle-class, but that doesn't necessarily make me bourgeois. How can I be bourgie when I own absolutely nothing, when I have crack-heads and jailbirds in my immediate family? Some folks attribute my being "different" to going to college. A lot of times being "educated" is equated with being bourgeois or highfa-lutin', as folks used to say. I don't think I'm either one, but there are people in my family who would beg to differ with me. I don't feel like they love me any less though.

For as long as I can remember my mother has had what other people in my family call "expen-sive taste." I have sort of the same reputation, only I'm real eva-sive about what I spend my money on. Sometimes I don't have the patience to wait for something to go on sale or to go through a sale rack, so I've been known to spend more for something than it's worth. In this, my mother trained me well. From her I learned that it's better to spend more money and have something longer than to buy cheap stuff you have to replace over and over. When I was in high school she talked me into spending a hun-dred and forty dollars on a pair of black leather Joan & David boots. My friends thought I had lost my mind. But the boots lasted me for eight years. My mother's into quality stuff, and to some people that's bourgie.

My family trips off everything from the way I dress to why I choose the "low maintenance" approach to my appearance, my eating habits, and anything else I do that is outside the norm for black folks. My grandmother still can't understand why I don't eat pork or red meat. She always lectures me about how she's been eating all that stuff for over fifty years and "ain't nothing wrong" with her. That red meat stays along the walls of your colon for months after it's consumed doesn't matter to her. Nor does the fact that pork causes hypertension and fried foods clog your arteries. Not one of my relatives can understand how I can eat a meal with no meat or why I take the skin off fried chicken. I would *really* get talked about if I brought pesto to one of our family gatherings or if I brought greens, the way I cook them, with smoked turkey parts. And if they knew that I spend five dollars on a bottle of pure maple syrup, they would all be *convinced* that I'm a basket case. I get ragged on for referring to turkey dressing as "stuffing." They already think I'm "white-acting," so when stuff like that pops out, it only confirms their ideas about me. To me stuffing and dressing are the same thing.

Angie, my mother's youngest sister, is forever going on about giving me a lesson on applying make-up. Every time I see her she teases me (in a serious kind of way) about how she's going to give me a make-over. She calls me "plain Jane" and doesn't understand that I don't mind looking plain. She cannot comprehend the notion that I actually *like* the way I look without make-up. And even though no one else bugs me about it the way she does, I get the feeling they're all thinking the same thing. It's that whole thing about "looking like a lady" or trying to enhance your appearance so you'll be ready when Mr. Right comes along, I guess. It just so happens that Angie is more verbal (or perhaps a little less sensitive) than everybody else. Or maybe, by now, they've all sort of figured me out and are letting me do my own thing, which is all I ever asked in the first place.

In terms of my self-image, there is something that I have yet to figure. Everybody knows that black folks are color conscious and a lot of horrible things go down in the black community about light-skin vs. dark-skin. I am sick and tired of hearing about it, and I would like to believe that as we approach the year 2000 this is an issue of the past.

> *I want to believe that with the resurgence of Afrocentrism and self-love in the black community, these issues no longer have a place in our community.*

Unfortunately, I think that I'm going to have to continue "wanting to believe."

My little episode with that woman and her sons was enough to convince me that it's far from being an issue of the past. One time I was on the bus, and I heard this young woman telling her friends that when she had her baby—before the doctor brought the baby to her —she was praying to God not to let her baby be too black. I could think of a hundred and one other things to be concerned about after just giving birth to a baby. I'm so grateful that in all of my little conflicts with myself and the way I look, being dark was never something that I hated about myself. My nose, hips, booty, hair, and the rest of my body, yes, but never my complexion, which I find pretty amazing considering that I come from a very southern, country (for lack of a better word) family.

 M y folks are from Louisiana, where as we all know, color is a major issue. But they have been in California for over fifty years. Not to sound like color ain't an issue here. My cousin D.C. is what folks call "red bones." We were raised together, and I can't remember ever being made to feel like I was any less pretty because I was dark and she was light. As a matter of fact, I can remember I was always being complimented on what a pretty little girl I was. Maybe that was their way of over-compensating, to make sure that I didn't grow up hating being dark. A lot of people develop a real bad complex about being dark. In my case, any confrontations that I have had about my complexion did not come from my family, but from other people. A boy in my junior high school said that I was too dark to wear red; that could be the reason that I still don't care much for red.

I've had people tell me that they were treated better or worse by heir family because of their complexion.

One of my Chicana friends told me how she was favored by her parents and considered prettier than her sister, because she was the fairest. As a result, she's now overly concerned about her appearance, in that weird, obsessive kind of way that I think white women are. I always tell her that *she* shouldn't be insecure, she's closer to what it means to be beautiful in America than I am. I think she understands what the "beauty" lie is all about. Of the two of us, if anybody should be insecure and freaking out about the way they look, it should be me, since everything in our society says beauty is the opposite of what I look like.

My family never did to me what millions of African Americans and, as my friend has proved, other folks do to their children. When I think how lucky I am not having endured those kinds of problems from my family, it makes it all worthwhile working a little harder to understand my kin folks and to help them understand me. Somehow it all balances out, makes it o.k. that they think I'm weird, a goody-two-shoes, and even bourgie.

I am definitely my mother's child: the kind of person I am and have been (*well* before I even met my mentors). Even though there are eighteen years between us, we share some very similar personality traits. My grandmother call us "the Siamese twins." Aside from looking exactly alike, she swears we have the same temperment. My mother is a kind, generous, and genuinely caring person. She enjoys giving and doing things for other people. She gives without expecting anything in return. I, on the other hand, expect to be paid back when I loan people money. Family or not!

three wise women

My extended family, the women who, since I was eighteen, have been to all of my birthday celebrations, graduations, and other special occasions have a lot in common despite their differences. There is something about me, at various stages in my life, that must have reminded them of their own "coming of age." It seems like everything I do, one of them has already done and usually has some words of wisdom to share with me. When I think of these women and their impact on my life, I think of the African proverb: *It takes an entire village to raise a child.* At my college graduation, I made this statement as I crossed the stage to receive my diploma: "Thanks to my family and friends for love and support, and a *special* thanks to Paulette, Elaine, and Joy for being such inspirational figures in my life."

If I had to choose the most influential people in my life, it would no doubt be these three women. In my teenage years we called them my "other mothers." It was cute then, but now they say I'm too old for that, so we've changed it to "big sisters." Even now, as I am rapidly approaching thirty, they are still my mentors, my role models, and my good friends. It's hard to imagine what my life would have been like if they had not been there to guide me and in some cases "push" me in the right direction. In this day and age, there are African-American young adults who need role models and extended families to assist them in making the right choices. It's rough growing up in America, and unless you have folks other than your parents taking an interest in you, the wrong path can become an easy option.

As black women, and as women period, we share the process of coming to terms with our beauty, appreciating it. At some time in our lives we've all felt ugly or absolutely hated some part of our body. It's hard to imagine that such beautiful, radiant women could have ever gone through such a period. My confidence and independence—two of my best character traits—can be attributed to these three women. Being self-sufficient, making my own way, is something that was ingrained in me from the beginning.

One of the first things I noticed about all of the women I grew to admire and respect is that they had their own homes, their own cars, and their own money. They were dependent on no one but themselves. They weren't married, and it was obvious that they didn't need to be taken care of or to have someone help them with the bills. It's a reality: some people get married for reasons other than love. Hooking up with someone for their money or someone who could show me the "finer things in life" is a thought I've never entertained. If anything, I always thought I'd have to deal with men who had dollar bill signs in their eyes when I told them what *I* did for a living, like Paulette.

Paulette told me what happened when men found out she was an electrician—making somewhere around twenty-five dollars an hour. Joy had to remind herself not to let it slip out that she owned her house (not to mention four others).

I have to be able to take care of myself, by myself. I honestly feel that I am totally deserving of nothing less than the best— although I have been known to settle, on occasion. I don't date a man just because he shows interest in me. I'm working at being the kind of woman who continues to have a balanced, productive, and happy existence regardless of whether or not she has a man around.

I could say that the three big sisters also can take the credit for my being an "old soul," but that's not true. Sometimes they tease me about acting older than they do. They don't find my taste in music entertaining at all. I'm always looking for a club that plays L.T.D.; Sly & The Family Stone; Earth, Wind & Fire; the Emotions; Ohio players; Isley Brothers—and the like. I love oldies but goodies, especially music from the seventies. Friends my own age bug off me too. Once I made the mistake of mentioning that we should have a James Brown party for my birthday. They looked at me like I had lost my mind. Shiree *still* caps on me for having a *Best of Con Funk Shun* tape.

I first met Paulette when I was thirteen. She was going to school to become an electrician's apprentice to my stepfather. We didn't get to be close friends until I was eighteen and traveled to Kenya together. She has always given me words to live by, encouraging me to think positively and not to underestimate myself. I've always been somewhat of a responsible person, but Paulette had more confidence in my ability to be responsible than my own parents. In my sophomore and junior years in college she let me house-sit for her when she took her two-month excursions to Egypt. I was all of 19 or 20 years old and completely responsible for her house and car. She left her entire belongings in my possession—even after I stuck a wooden spoon down her three hundred dollar Champion juicer. I've never really understood why she had so much confidence in me, but I paid the bills, made bank deposits, collected the rent from her tenants, and basically maintained her household in her absence. A product of the "age of Aquarius," Paulette would be the kind of laid back, nonjudgemental parent who would let her children learn from their life's experiences. My mother taught me how to drive a stick shift, but I used Paulette's car to practice and perfect it. She would be the kind of parent who would be "friends" with her children.

When we were going to Africa, to Kenya, I think she knew better than my mother that I didn't need a tight reign. (I still wonder what possessed her to invite an eighteen year old on vacation with her.) It was as though she knew the kind of effect such a trip would have on my life before we left. By the end of the trip I had her using all my Berkeley High slang terms. Paulette is somewhat of a "resource" person for me. She bought me my first copy of *Our Bodies, Ourselves* for my sixteenth birthday. I can talk to her about any and everything. She doesn't expect perfection. She lectures me, but not in the same way most folks do. She gives me credit for being somewhat of an intelligent person. Whenever I need someone to talk to, Paulette is the first person I call. I am sometimes reluctant to tell some of my other friends about my romantic interludes, because I get the feeling that in their sisters-sitting-around-the-table talks they would discuss my affairs and judge me, making all kinds of assumptions about me on that basis. I don't get that feeling from Paulette, so I tell her everything. The only thing she is concerned with, when it comes to men, is whether or not I used a condom, and if I had a good time.

I can never slip anything by her. I get busted every time. She fills me with common sense advice, and I often find myself saying, "Paulette said...." She tells me things like: "Don't burn any bridges," or "Don't worry about things until you have to," or, "There are some things you don't have any control over, be concerned with the things you *can* control."

For Valentine's Day one year while I was in New York, she sent me a huge box with dozens of homemade chocolate chip cookies wrapped in a cloth napkin. I was confused when I opened the care package of Al-Anon and Adult Children of Alcoholic reading material since I wasn't an alcoholic nor the child of one. The note enclosed with the booklets read:

Dear Aliona,
Hope you had a good cross country trip.
Since you're in the mood to get mad at
folks, I figured you might as well get
mad at me. I should have given you this
stuff a while ago. You have to realize that
you are setting up patterns of behavior
that will undermine your success. You're
not doing it by yourself or on purpose. Past
programming is giving you a hand you don't
want. The hard part is that you have to
make the change but you don't have to do
it alone. You have me, Joy, Elaine, Melody
(all ACAs) and Al-Anon (it's nationwide).
Remember what we say to you might sound
like criticism and negativity, but it's because
we love you, have been there before and don't
want to see you hurt where it can be avoided.
I know your mouth is poked out, so enough
for now. We'll talk soon.

Love & Stuff,

Paulette

She was right, again. My mouth was poked out, about some trivial shit that I can't even remember.

Paulette's mother is a local celebrity in Boston. She is retired from Boston College as the Director of the black studies program. She received a graduate degree from Harvard after raising her two daughters and countless surrogate sons. I read an article about her in a Boston paper, where she mentioned how she always encouraged her children to pursue a career in something they enjoyed. To me, this was unheard of. Most folks I know are too concerned with just getting a job. I was expected to be content with a job that had health and dental benefits. Deep down, I've always known that it would take a little more than those things to keep me happily employed, but, of course I never dared mention it. In a sense, Paulette's mother encouraged her girls to reach for the stars, and Paulette has always made me feel that if I tried hard enough, there was nothing I couldn't do, much like her mother must have told her students at Boston College.

I don't think becoming an electrician was something she ever thought was beyond her grasp. After giving college a try, she enrolled in an apprenticeship program to become one of the first black women to join local 595. The fact that she was about to enter a field that was predominately white and even more white-male dominated didn't discourage her from giving it a shot. She made a lot of money and enjoyed her work. The trade-off was that she had to deal with overt sexism *and* racism on a grand scale and on a daily basis. By the time she left the union she had been called a bitch by her boss and was receiving sexually explicit notes left on her car windshield. Me? I would have been gone the first time I showed up at work (where I was the only woman) and found a *Penthouse* picture of a woman, with her legs open, posted on the wall.

I met Elaine through Paulette, when we travelled to Kenya together. We spent a week in the Virgin Islands too: Paulette, Elaine, my mother, and me. In St. Thomas Elaine saved my life when I panicked and began inhaling water. She's an excellent swimmer, and in my attempt to go snorkeling in water over my head, she supported me with one hand and emptied the water from my face mask with the other. She's about three or four inches shorter than I am, but way more shapely. She's in much better shape than I am too. She has been swimming regularly, for over ten years swimming no less than seventy-two laps at a time. I can't do seventy-two of anything. She has what one would call a "balanced" lifestyle, an advocate of caring for the mind, body and soul. Without make-up and being all dressed up, she looks more like my peer than someone closer to my mother's age, especially when she had her braces or when she wears braids.

My first trip to northern California to a health spa for a mud bath was with Elaine. She encouraged me to take the day off and pamper myself. So I agreed to join her, Joy and another friend visiting from Michigan. It was nothing new for Elaine, she goes to Calistoga for the works every three months. (They know her on a first name basis.) I was a little intimidated by the long, deep tub of heated mud. I couldn't help but think of what was at the bottom of the tub, just how deep it was, or what would happen if I started to sink down too far. I wanted to know if it was like quick sand, but I was too embarassed to ask. Once I got in, all of those worries quickly disappeared. Two minutes of being covered up to my neck in that mud, and I didn't care how deep it was or even if it *was* like quick sand. By the end of the two and a half hours I felt like a noodle and more relaxed than I can ever remember feeling. After that we went for lunch at a fancy restaurant, followed by wine tasting at a couple of wineries. It was the best Monday I've ever had in my life. On the way home, I thought to myself: And she's always saying how wonderful it is having *me* in her life!.

Elaine, more than anybody else, is in *total* support of my desire to throw my stuff in storage and hit the road. She always tells me that you have to ask for what you want in life, put it out there, and the universe will take care of the rest.

The common rap by brothers in California and their preference for women of other races is that we don't like to do "certain things" that they like to do. You know, clean, healthy stuff like skiing, white water rafting, camping, water skiing. Well, Elaine does all of that. She's carmel-colored brown, which becomes a nice golden tan color if she's been kicking it in the Carribean. She *looks* the part for California men, having hair well past her shoulders. But the minute she opens her mouth and they find out how smart she is, they scram.

A strange thing happened between Elaine and me. I went out a couple of times with a guy that she had dated. I didn't know it until after I started seeing him. When I found out he knew her, naturally I had to call her up and get the 411 on him, and, of course, she broke it down. I thought it was such a neat thing, because there was no hostility on either side, and, as I later found out, the guy was not worthy of any. If she had a problem with it (she wouldn't have, she's way too deep for that), I would have dropped him like a hot potato. No man is worth jeopardizing my relationship with any of my friends.

I tell Elaine all kinds of stuff about my personal affairs with the hope of her sharing her "words of wisdom" with me. She told me a long time ago that if sex with a man was bad, don't do it again. She would even stop seeing someone if sex was bad. At first, I thought it was kind of harsh. I'm sure I must have said something like, "What if he's a nice guy?" She said matter-of-factly, "Keep him as a friend." That it was obviously something she had given a lot of thought to.

Now, a few years later, I see what she means. To Elaine, under no uncertain terms should a woman stay in a relationship where her needs, in any capacity, are not being met. Elaine would be the first to say that she is no expert on relationships, but since she has been around a few years longer than me, I could learn from her mistakes and not make the same ones myself. Her sharing insights with me is a true sign of affection and love.

A serious business person is one who can separate business from pleasure and not be a bitch at the same time. Joy is a serious business woman. I worked for her for a while, and we became friends. I feel a special kind of closeness with her, especially since we nearly met our judgment day together.

I met Joy nearly ten years ago, around the time I met Elaine. We have a good time and talk, but I tell her things sometimes in a kind of round-a-bout way. Of the three, Joy gives me the least amount of sympathy. It's almost as though she's taken a business approach to how she chooses to live her life, and for her it has paid off. Joy is very successful. She's a buppie—only smarter. She did her undergraduate and graduate work at the University of Massachussettes at Amherst. If I had followed her footsteps I would be done with graduate school, have a masters degree, and not be freaking out about taking the G.R.E. right now. She encourages me to take a practical approach to things and most of all to *think* about what I want to do before trying to do it. I know that if by the time I'm thirty my life is still in shambles, I will definitely hear about it from Joy.

Joy represents for me the importance of financial stability and the ability to manage money. She's also represents the great American work ethic: Work hard now, so you won't have to later. While everyone else was travelling around the world, Joy was saving her money, and four years ago bought a small retail business. Her store is in a yuppie part of Oakland and does very well. She has one of the two black-owned businesses in the area, the only African-American woman who does, in addition to starting a scholarship at a local high school in honor of her late mother. In between dealing with corporate America, successfully running her business, managing her properties, having a social life and a significant other, she somehow made time to become a big sister to a young black girl. Even though she doesn't have any children of her own, somehow she still felt the need to become a positive role model in someone else's life. I admire her dedication and committment.

I interviewed Joy, the successful businesswoman, for my senior thesis, and she told me that she was encouraged to excell in school to compensate for not being cute. Her story was not unlike others that a lot of brown-skinned girls had to deal with growing up. I was amazed when she shared her experiences about racism in corporate America and her problems with other blacks in the work place. She told me about young black women who preferred taking orders from a white person rather than from her. They decided that she was white-washed and needed some black culture in her life. Listening to her stories, I found myself pondering the question, once more: What makes a person who is *not* confused about who they are or where they came from, and definitely knows where they're going, an oreo? There is nothing "white" about the kind of woman Joy is. She's a smart, serious, successful, goal-oriented black woman who has learned what it takes to succeed in a white man's world. She's learned their game and has proven that, when given the opportunity, she can give them a run for their money. Joy is my common/business sense mentor and keeps me on the straight and narrow.

...and me

I t's amazing to me that none of these three women has been married. I always thought they were everything that would make a woman more appealing to a man: smart, assertive, successful, and independent. As odd as it may sound, it's possible to be too smart or too successful (and thus too threatening) for some brothers. It really doesn't say a whole lot for the brothers out there, because my friends are not the exception. So when the *Oakland Tribune* ran a story (on the front page of the Sunday edition, no less) that Oakland was rated as one of the top ten places in the country to meet black men, I nearly had a fit! I sat down and wrote a letter to the Editor. I was speaking on behalf of myself and my friends. I broke it down, which basically dis'd Oakland and the brothers—*and* I signed my first and last name. Wouldn't you know, my letter got published! The editor in chief at the time was a black woman. She probably knew exactly what I was talking about. At first, I was embarrassed. Then I realized that everything I wrote was the truth: In the letter, I explained that I was speaking from personal experience since I was born and raised in Oakland. I wrote that before I moved to the east coast my interaction with black men was practically nonexistent, and that any chances I may have had with the brothers was completely diminshed when I began to wear my hair in a short natural. Basically, I made the point that unless a woman fits the mold— a size eight or under—she could hang up the idea of attracting black men in the Bay Area. Not to mention the fact that even if she *does* fit the mold, a lot of the black men in the Bay Area just don't like black women. I recalled telling a girlfriend visiting from the midwest not to be surprised if the brothers ignored her at the Latin music club, where we went for salsa lessons. She thought I was exaggerating until she got in the class and the only other black person there was a brother who chose to sit out a round rather than partner her. In closing the letter, I added that I had friends who were doctors, lawyers, accountants, electricians, artists, entrepreneurs, etc., who had been in the Bay Area for ten and fifteen years and hadn't found Mr. Right. So my advice to any black woman moving out west would be to bring your man with you.

My friends are prime examples of what I was trying to say in my letter. It amazes me that they are still single. Melody, who moved back to New York, has the love story of the century, and lends credence to the theory that the best things happen when you least expect them. She had pretty much given up the idea of marriage. She had so thoroughly accepted the fact that she would probably spend the rest of her life alone that she bought a cute, little house on Long Island. The minute she moved in and got comfortable she met her fiancé. Her wedding is at the end of the year.

In helping to shape and mold me, these women are doing what black women have done since day one.

> *Despite the obstacles and the ups and downs of being a black woman in a racist and sexist world, we have managed to make a place for ourselves.*

We are the descendants of slaves, many of them survivors of sexual, physical and emotional abuse, yet we manage to keep on keeping on, just like the many heroic and triumphant black women before us and the ones who will come after us.

Over the years I've gotten something very special from each of the women who served as mentors to me. They had a greater impact on my life than any of us could have imagined. I guess I've been the child they never had, and they, in turn, have given me the closeness of a mother/daughter relationship that I never had (but haven't given up on) with my real mother. I think there's a little bit of each—Paulette, Elaine, Joy, and Melody—in me. I'm tickled by the thought, because that would make me one hell of a woman.